Folle-Farine, by 'Ouida'.

by Marie Louise De La Ramée

Address:
HardPress
8345 NW 66TH ST #2561
MIAMI FL 33166-2626
USA
Email: info@hardpress.net

FOLLE-FARINE.

FOLLE-FARINE.

Novels

BY OUIDA,

AUTHOR OF "UNDER TWO FLAGS," "PUCK," "TRICOTRIN," ETC.

" Un gazetier fumeux qui se croit un flambeau
  Dit au pauvre qu'il a noyé dans les ténèbres :
  Où donc l'aperçois-tu ce Créateur du Beau ?
  Ce Rédresseur que tu célèbres ? "   BAUDELAIRE.

IN THREE VOLUMES.

VOL. I.

LONDON :

CHAPMAN & HALL, 193, PICCADILLY.

1871.

250 . ℔ 174.

LONDON
BRADBURY, EVANS, AND CO., PRINTERS, WHITEFRIARS.

A

𝕷𝔞 𝕸𝔢𝔪𝔬𝔦𝔯𝔢

D'INGRES.

𝔢𝔦𝔫𝔱𝔯𝔢.——𝕷𝔬ë𝔱𝔢.

BOOK I.

DUST.

FOLLE-FARINE.

CHAPTER I.

NOT the wheat itself; not even so much as the chaff; only the dust from the corn. The dust which no one needs or notices; the mock farina which flies out from under the two revolving circles of the grindstones; the impalpable cloud which goes forth to gleam golden in the sun a moment, and then is scattered; on the wind; into the water; up in the sunlight; down in the mud: what matters? who cares?

Only the dust: a mote in the air; a speck in the light; a black spot in the living daytime; a colourless atom in the immensity of the atmos-

phere, borne up one instant to gleam against the
sky, dropped down the next to lie in a fetid ditch.

Only the dust: the dust that flows out from
between the grindstones, grinding exceeding hard
and small, as the religion which calls itself Love
avers that its God does grind the world.

"It is a nothing, less than nothing. The stones
turn; the dust is born; it has a puff of life; it
dies. Who cares? No one. Not the good God;
not any man; not even the devil. It is a thing
even devil-deserted. Ah, it is very like you," said
the old miller, watching the mill-stones.

Folle-Farine heard—she had heard a hundred
times,—and held her peace.

Folle-Farine: the dust; only the dust.

As good a name as any other for a nameless
creature. The dust;—sharp-winnowed and rejected
of all, as less worthy than even the shred husks and
the shattered stalks.

Folle-Farine,—she watched the dust fly in and
out all day long from between the grindstones.
She only wondered why, if she and the dust were
thus kindred and namesakes, the wind flew away
with the dust so mercifully, and yet never would
fly away with her.

The dust was carried away by the breeze, and

wandered wherever it listed. The dust had a sweet short summer-day life of its own ere it died. If it were worthless, it at least was free. It could lie in the curl of a green leaf, or on the white breast of a flower. It could mingle with the golden dust in a lily, and almost seem to be one with it. It could fly with the thistledown, and with the feathers of the dandelion, on every roving wind that blew.

In a vague, dreamy fashion, the child wondered why the dust was so much better dealt with than she was.

"Folle-Farine! Folle—Folle—Folle—Farine!" the other children hooted after her, echoing the name by which the grim humour of her bitter-tongued taskmaster had called her. She had got used to it, and answered to it as others to their birth-names.

It meant that she was a thing utterly useless, absolutely worthless; the very refuse of the winnowings of the flail of fate. But she accepted that too, so far as she understood it; she only sometimes wondered in a dull fierce fashion why, if she and the dust were sisters, the dust had its wings whilst she had none.

All day long the dust flew in and out and about

as it liked, through the open doors, and among the tossing boughs, and through the fresh cool mists, and down the golden shafts of the sunbeams; and all day long she stayed in one place and toiled, and was first beaten and then cursed, or first cursed and then beaten,—which was all the change that her life knew. For herself, she saw no likeness betwixt her and the dust; for that escaped from the scourge and flew forth, but she abode under the flail, always.

Nevertheless, Folle-Farine was all the name she knew.

The great black wheel churned and circled in the brook water, and lichens and ferns and mosses made lovely all the dark, shadowy, silent place; the red mill roof gleamed in the sun, under a million summer leaves; the pigeons came and went all day in and out of their holes in the wall; the sweet scents of ripening fruits in many orchards filled the air; the great grindstones turned and turned and turned, and the dust floated forth to dance with the gnat and to play with the sunbeam.

Folle-Farine sat aloft, on the huge wet timbers above the wheel, and watched with her great sorrowful eyes, and wondered again, after her own

fashion, why her namesake had th
forth whilst she had none.

Suddenly a shrill screaming voice broke the
stillness savagely.

" Little devil ! " cried the miller, " go fetch me
those sacks, and carry them within, and pile
them ; neatly, do you hear ? Like the piles of
stone in the road."

Folle-Farine swung down from the timbers in
obedience to the command, and went to the heap of
sacks that lay outside the mill ; small sacks, most
of them ; all of last year's flour.

There was an immense gladiolus growing near, in
the mill-garden, where they were ; a tall flower all
scarlet and gold, and straight as a palm, with bees
sucking into its bells, and butterflies poising on its
stem. She stood a moment looking at its beauty;
she was scarce any higher than its topmost bud, and
was in her way beautiful, something after its fashion.
She was a child of six or eight years, with limbs
moulded like sculpture, and brown as the brook
water ; great lustrous eyes, half savage and half
soft ; a mouth like a red pomegranate bud, and
straight dark brows—the brows of the friezes of
Egypt.

Her only clothing was a little short white linen

kirtle, knotted around her waist, and falling to her knees; and her skin was burned, by exposure in the sun, to a golden brown colour, though in texture it was soft as velvet, and showed all the veins like glass. Standing there in the deep grass, with the scarlet flower against her, and purple butter-flies over her head, an artist would have painted her and called her by a score of names, and described for her some mystical or noble fate : as Anteros, perhaps, or as the doomed son of Procne, or as some child born to the Forsaken in the savage forests of Naxos, or conceived by Perse-phone, in the eternal night of hell, whilst still the earth lay black and barren and fruitless, under the ban and curse of a bereaved maternity.

But here she had only one name, Folle-Farine ; and here she had only to labour drearily and stupidly, like the cattle of the field, and without their strength, and with barely so much even as their scanty fare and begrudged bed.

The sunbeams that fell on her might find out that she had a beauty which ripened and grew rich under their warmth, like that of a red flower bud or a golden autumn fruit. But nothing else ever did. In none of the eyes that looked on her had she any sort of loveliness. She was Folle-Farine ; a little wicked beast that only merited at best a whip and a cruel word, a broken crust and a malediction; a thing born of the devil, and out of which the devil needed to be scourged incessantly.

The sacks were all small; they were the property of the peasant proprietors of the district : the department of Calvados. But though small they were heavy in proportion to her age and power. She lifted one, although with effort, yet with the familiarity of an accustomed action; poised it on her back, clasped it tight with her round slender arms, and carried it slowly through the open door of the mill. That one put down upon the bricks, she came for a second,—a third,—a fourth,—a fifth,—a sixth, working doggedly, patiently and willingly, as a little donkey works.

The sacks were in all sixteen; before the seventh she paused.

It was a hot day in the late summer: she was panting and burning with the exertion; the bloom in her cheeks had deepened to scarlet; she stood a moment, resting, bathing her face in the sweet coolness of a white tall tuft of lilies.

The miller looked round where he worked, amongst his beans and cabbages, and saw.

"Little mule! Little beast!" he cried. "Would

you be lazy—you!—who have no more right to
live at all than an eft, or a stoat, or a toad!"

And as he spoke he came towards her. He had
caught up a piece of rope with which he had been
about to tie his beans to a stake, and he struck
the child with it. The sharp cord bit the flesh
cruelly, curling round her bare chest and shoulders,
and leaving a livid mark.

She quivered a little, but she said nothing; she
lifted her head and looked at him, and dropped her
hands to her sides. Her eyes glowed fiercely;
her red curling lips shut tight; her straight brows
drew together.

"Little devil! Will you work now?" said the
miller. "Do you think you are to stand in the sun
and smell at flowers—you! Pouf-f-f!"

Folle-Farine did not move.

"Pick up the sacks this moment, little brute,"
said the miller. "If you stand still a second before
they are all housed, you shall have as many stripes
as there are sacks left untouched. Oh, hè: do you
hear?"

She heard, but she did not move.

"Do you hear," he pursued. "As many strokes
as there are sacks; little wretch. Now—I will give
you three moments to choose. One!"

Folle-Farine still stood mute and immovable, her head erect, her arms crossed on her chest. A small, slender, bronze-hued, half-nude figure amongst the ruby hues of the gladioli and the pure snow-like whiteness of the lilies.

" Two ! "

She stood in the same attitude, the sacks lying untouched at her feet, a purple-winged butterfly lighting on her head.

" Three ! "

She was still mute ; still motionless.

He seized her by the shoulder with one hand, and with the other lifted the rope.

It curled round her breast and back, again and again and again; she shuddered, but she did not utter a single cry. He struck her the ten times ; with the same number of strokes as there remained sacks uncarried. He did not exert any great strength, for had he used his uttermost he would have killed her, and she was of value to him ; but he scourged her with a merciless exactitude in the execution of his threat, and the rope was soon wet with drops of her bright young blood.

The noonday sun fell golden all around ; the deep sweet peace of the silent country reigned everywhere ; the pigeons fled to and fro in and out of their little arched homes ; the millstream flowed on, singing a pleasant song; now and then a ripe apricot dropped with a low sound on the turf ; close about was all the radiance of summer flowers ; of heavy rich roses, of yellow lime tufts, of sheaves of old-fashioned comely phlox, and all the delicate shafts of the graceful lilies. And in the warmth the child shuddered under the scourge ; against the light the black rope curled like a serpent darting to sting ; among the sun-fed blossoms there fell a crimson stain.

But never a word had she uttered. She endured to the tenth stroke in silence.

He flung the cord aside amongst the grass. "Daughter of devils ! — what strength the devil gives !" he muttered.

Folle-Farine said nothing. Her face was livid, her back bruised and lacerated, her eyes still glanced with undaunted scorn and untamed passion. Still she said nothing ; but, as his hand released her, she darted as noiselessly as a lizard to the water's edge, set her foot on the lowest range of the wood-work, and in a second leaped aloft to the highest point, and seated herself astride on that crossbar of timber on which she had been throned when he had summoned her first, above the foam of the churning wheels, and in the deepest shadow of innumerable leaves.

Then she lifted up a voice as pure, as strong, as fresh as the voice of a mavis in May time, and sang, with reckless indifference, a stave of song in a language unknown to any of the people of that place; a loud fierce air, with broken words of curious and most dulcet melody, which rang loud and defiant, yet melancholy, even in their rebellion, through the foliage, and above the sound of the loud mill water.

"It is a chaunt to the foul fiend," the miller muttered to himself. "Well, why does he not come and take his own; he would be welcome to it." And he went and sprinkled holy water on his rope, and said an ave or two over it to exorcise it.

Every fibre of her childish body ached and throbbed; the stripes on her shoulders burned like flame; her little brain was dizzy; her little breast was black with bruises; but still she sang on, clutching the timber with her hands to keep her from falling into the foam below, and flashing her proud eyes down through the shade of the leaves.

"Can one never cut the devil out of her?" muttered the miller, going back to his work amongst the beans.

After a while the song ceased; the pain she suffered stifled her voice despite herself; she felt giddy and sick, but she sat there still in the shadow, holding on by the jutting woodwork, and watching the water foam and eddy below.

The hours went away; the golden day died; the greyness of evening stole the glow from the gladioli and shut up the buds of the roses; the lilies gleamed but the whiter in the dimness of twilight; the vesper chimes were rung from the cathedral two leagues away over the fields.

The miller stopped the gear of the mill; the grindstones and the water-wheels were set at rest; the peace of the night came down; the pigeons flew to roost in their niches; but the sacks still lay uncarried on the grass, and a spider had found time to spin his fairy ropes about them.

The miller stood on his threshold, and looked up at her where she sat aloft in the dusky shades of the leaves.

"Come down and carry these sacks, little brute," he said. "If not—no supper for you to-night."

Folle-Farine obeyed him and came down from the huge pile, slowly, her hands crossed behind her back, her head erect, her eyes glancing like the eyes of a wild hawk.

She walked straight past the sacks, across the dew-laden turf, through the tufts of the lilies, and so silently into the house.

The entrance was a wide kitchen, paved with blue and white tiles, clean as a watercress, filled with the pungent odour of dried herbs, and furnished with brass pots and pans, with walnut presses, with pinewood tressels, and with strange little quaint pictures and images of saints. On one of the tressels were set a jug of steaming milk, some rolls of black bread, and a big dish of stewed cabbages. At the meal there was already seated a lean, brown, wrinkled, careworn old serving woman, clad in the blue kirtle and the white head gear of Normandy.

The miller stayed the child at the threshold.

"Little devil—not a bit nor drop to-night if you do not carry the sacks."

Folle-Farine said nothing, but moved on, past the food on the board, past the images of the saints, past the high lancet window, through which the moonlight had begun to stream, and out at the opposite door.

There she climbed a steep winding stairway on to which that door had opened, pushed aside a little wooden wicket, entered a loft in the roof, loosened the single garment that she wore, shook it off from her, and plunged into the fragrant mass of daisied hay and of dry orchard mosses which served her as a bed. Covered in these, and curled like a dormouse in its nest, she clasped her hands above her head, and sought to forget in sleep her hunger and her wounds. She was well used to both.

Below there was a crucifix, with a bleeding God upon it; there was a little rudely sculptured representation of the Nativity; there was a wooden figure of St. Christopher; a portrait of the Madonna, and many other symbols of the church. But the child went to her bed without a prayer on her lips, and with a curse on her head, and bruises on her body.

Sleep, for once, would not come to her. She was too hurt and sore to be able to lie without pain; the dried grasses, so soft to her usually, were like thorns beneath the skin that still swelled and smarted from the stripes of the rope. She was feverish; she tossed and turned in vain; she suffered too much to be still; she sat up and stared with her passionate wistful eyes, at the leaves that were swaying against the square casement in the .

wall, and the moonbeam that shone so cold and bright across her bed.

She listened, all her senses awake, to the noises of the house. They were not many: a cat's mew, a mouse's scratch, the click-clack of the old woman's step, the shrill monotony of the old man's voice, these were all. After a while even these ceased; the wooden shoes clattered up the wooden stairs, the house became quite still; there was only in the silence the endless flowing murmur of the water breaking against the motionless wheels of the mill.

Neither man nor woman had come near to bring her anything to eat or drink. She had heard them muttering their prayers before they went to rest, but no hand unlatched her door. She had no disappointment, because she had had no hope. She had rebellion, because Nature had grafted it in her; but she went no further. She did not know what it was to hope. She was only a young wild animal, well used to blows, and drilled by them, but not tamed.

As soon as the place was silent, she got out of her nest of grass, slipped on her linen skirt, and opened her casement — a small square hole in the wall, and merely closed by a loose deal shutter, with a hole cut in it, scarcely bigger than her head. A delicious sudden rush of summer air met her burning face ; a cool cluster of foliage hit her a soft blow across the eyes as the wind stirred it. They were enough to allure her.

Like any other young cub of the woods, she had only two instincts—air and liberty.

She thrust herself out of the narrow window with the agility that only is born of frequent custom, and got upon the shelving thatch of a shed which sloped a foot or so below, slid down the roof, and swung herself by the jutting bricks of the outhouse wall on to the grass. The house dog, a brindled mastiff, that roamed loose all night about the mill, growled and sprang at her; then, seeing who she was, put up his gaunt head and licked her face, and turned again to resume the rounds of his vigilant patrol.

Ere he went, she caught and kissed him, closely and fervently, without a word. The mastiff was the only living thing that did not hate her; she was grateful, in a passionate, dumb, unconscious fashion. Then she took to her feet, ran, as swiftly as she could, along the margin of the water, and leaped like a squirrel into the wood, on whose edge the millhouse stood.

Once there she was content.

The silence, the shadows, the darkness where the
trees stood thick, the pale quivering luminance of
the moon, the mystical eërie sounds that fill a woodland by night, all which would have had terror for
tamer and happier creatures of her years, had only
for her a vague entranced delight. Nature had
made her without one pulse of fear; and she
had remained too ignorant to have been ever
taught it.

It was still warm with all the balmy breath of mid-
summer; there were heavy dews everywhere; here
and there on the surface of the water, there gleamed
the white closed cups of the lotus; through the
air there passed, now and then, the soft, grey, dim
body of a night-bird on the wing; the wood, whose
trees were pines, and limes, and maples, was
full of a deep dreamy odour; the mosses that
clothed many of the branches hung, film-
like, in the wind in lovely coils and web-like
phantasies.

Around stretched the vast country, dark and
silent, as in a trance, the stillness only broken by
some faint note of a sheep's bell, some distant song
of a mule-driver passing homeward.

The child strayed onward through the trees, in-
sensibly soothed, and made glad, she knew not

why, by all the dimness and the fragrance round her.

She stood up to her knees in the shallow freshets that every now and then broke up through the grasses; she felt the dews, shaken off the leaves above, fall deliciously upon her face and hair; she filled her hands with the night-blooming marvel-flower, and drank in its sweetness as though it were milk and honey; she crouched down and watched her own eyes look back at her from the dark gliding water of the river.

Then she threw herself on her back upon the mosses—so cool and moist that they seemed like balm upon the bruised hot skin—and lay there looking upward at the swift mute passage of the flitting owls, at the stately flight of the broad-winged moths, at the movement of the swift brown bats, at the soft trembling of the foliage in the breeze, at the great clouds slowly sailing across the brightness of the moon. All these things were infinitely sweet to her with the sweetness of free-dom, of love, of idleness, of rest, of all things which her life had never known: so dumbly may the young large-eyed antelope feel the beauty of the forest in the hot lull of tropic nights, when the speed of the pursuer has relaxed, and the aromatic breath of the panther is no more against its flank.

She lay there long, quite motionless, tracing, with a sort of voluptuous delight, all movements in the air, all changes in the clouds, all shadows in the leaves. All the immense multitude of ephemeral life which, unheard in the day, fills the earth with innumerable whispering voices after the sun has set, now stirred in every herb and under every bough around her.

The silvery ghost-like wing of an owl touched her forehead once. A little dormouse ran across her feet. Strange shapes floated across the cold white surface of the water. Quaint things, hairy, filmy-winged, swam between her and the stars. But none of these things had terror for her; they were things of the night, with which she felt vaguely the instinct of kinship.

She was only a little wild beast, they said, the offspring of darkness, and vileness, and rage and disgrace. And yet, in a vague imperfect way, the glories of the night, its mysterious and solemn beauty, its melancholy and lustrous charm, quenched the fierceness in her dauntless eyes, and filled them with dim wondering tears, and stirred the half dead soul in her to some dull pain, some nameless ecstacy, that were not merely physical.

And then, in her way, being stung by these, and moved, she knew not why, to a strange sad sense of loneliness and shame, and knowing no better she prayed.

She raised herself on her knees, and crossed her hands upon her chest, and prayed after the fashion that she had seen men and women and children pray at roadside shrines and crosses ; prayed aloud, with a little beating breaking heart, like the young child she was.

" Oh Devil ! if I be indeed thy daughter, stay with me ; leave me not alone : lend me thy strength and power, and let me inherit of thy kingdom. Give me this, oh great Lord, and I will praise thee and love thee always."

She prayed in all earnestness, in all simplicity, in broken, faltering language ; knowing no better ; knowing only that she was alone on the earth and friendless, and very hungry and in sore pain, whilst this mighty unknown King of the dominion of darkness, whose child she ever heard she was, had lost her, or abandoned her ; and reigned afar in some immortal world, oblivious of her misery.

The silence of the night alone gave back the echo

of her own voice. She waited breathless for some answer, for some revelation, some reply; there only came the pure cold moon, sailing straight from out a cloud, and striking on the waters.

She rose sadly to her feet, and went back along the shining course of the stream, through the grasses and the mosses, and under the boughs, to her little nest under the eaves.

As she left the obscurity of the wood and passed into the fuller light, her bare feet glistening, and her shoulders wet with the showers of dew, a large dark shape flying down the wind smote her with his wings upon the eyes, lighted one moment on her head, and then swept onward lost in shade. At that moment, likewise, a radiant golden globe flashed to her sight, dropped to her footsteps, and shone an instant in the glisten from the skies.

It was but a great goshawk seeking for its prey; it was but a great meteor fading and falling at its due appointed hour; but to the heated, savage, dreamy fancy of the child it seemed an omen, an answer, a thing of prophecy, a spirit of air; nay, why not Him himself?

In legends, which had been the only lore her ears had ever heard, it had been often told he took such shapes as this.

"If he should give me his kingdom!" she
thought; and her eyes flashed alight; her heart
swelled; her cheeks burned. The little dim un-
tutored brain could not hold the thought long or
close enough to grasp, or sift, or measure it; but
some rude rich glory, impalpable, unutterable,
seemed to come to her and bathe her in its heat
and colour. She was his offspring, so they all told
her; why not, then, also his heir?

She felt, as felt the goatherd or the charcoal-
burner in those legends she had fed on, who was
suddenly called from poverty and toil, from hunger
and fatigue, from a fireless hearth and a bed of
leaves, to inherit some fairy empire, to ascend to
some region of the gods.

Like one of these, hearing the summons to some
great unknown imperial power smite all his poor
pale barren life to splendour, so Folle-Farine,
standing by the water's side in the light of the
moon, desolate, ignorant, brute-like, felt elected to
some mighty heritage unseen of men. If this were
waiting for her in the future, what matter, now,
were stripes or wounds or woe?

She smiled a little, dreamily, like one who beholds
fair visions in his sleep, and stole back over the
starlit grass, and swung herself upward by the

tendrils of ivy, and crouched once more down in her nest of mosses.

And either the courage of the spirits of darkness, or the influence of instincts dumb but nascent, was with her; for she fell asleep in her little loft in the roof as though she were a thing cherished of heaven and earth, and dreamed happily all through the hours of the slowly-rising dawn : her bruised body and her languid brain and her aching heart all stilled and soothed, and her hunger and passion and pain forgotten; with the night-blooming flowers still clasped in her hands, and on her closed mouth a smile.

For she dreamed of her Father's kingdom, a kingdom which no man denies to the creature that has beauty and youth, and is poor and yet proud, and is of the sex of its mother.

CHAPTER II.

IN one of the most fertile and most fair districts of northern France there was a little Norman town, very, very old and beautiful exceedingly by reason of its ancient streets, its high peaked roofs, its marvellous galleries and carvings, its exquisite greys and browns, its silence and its colour, and its rich still life.

Its centre was a great cathedral, noble as York or Chartres; a cathedral, whose spire shot to the clouds, and whose innumerable towers and pinnacles were all pierced to the day, so that the blue sky shone and the birds of the air flew all through them. A slow brown river, broad enough for market boats and for corn barges, stole through the place to the sea, lapping as it went the wooden piles of the houses, and reflecting the quaint shapes of the carvings, the hues of the signs and the draperies, the dark spaces of the dormer windows, the bright heads of some casement-cluster of carnations, the laughing face of a girl leaning out to smile on her lover.

All around it lay the deep grass unshaven, the leagues on leagues of fruitful orchards, the low blue hills tenderly interlacing one another, the fields of colza, where the white head-dress of the women workers flashed in the sun like a silvery pigeon's wing. To the west there were the deep green woods, and the wide plains golden with gorse of Arthur's and of Merlin's lands; and beyond, to the northward, was the dim stretch of the ocean breaking on a yellow shore, whither the river ran, and whither led straight shady roads, hidden with linden and with poplar trees, and marked ever and anon by a wayside wooden Christ, or by a little murmuring well crowned with a crucifix.

A beautiful, old, shadowy, ancient place: picturesque everywhere; often silent, with a sweet sad silence that was chiefly broken by the sound of bells or the chaunting of choristers. A place of the Middle Ages still. With lanterns swinging on cords from house to house as the only light;

with wondrous scroll-works and quaint signs
at the doors of all its traders; with monks'
cowls and golden croziers and white-robed
acolytes in its streets; with the subtle smoke of
incense coming out from the cathedral door to
mingle with the odours of the fruits and flowers in
the market-place; with great flat-bottomed boats
drifting down the river under the leaning eaves of
its dwellings; and with the galleries of its opposing
houses touching so nearly that a girl leaning in one
could stretch a Provence rose or toss an Easter
egg across to her neighbour in the other.

Doubtless, there were often squalor, poverty,
dust, filth, and uncomeliness within these old and
beautiful homes. Doubtless often the dwellers
therein were housed like cattle and slept like pigs,
and looked but once out to the woods and waters of
the landscapes round for one hundred times that
they looked at their hidden silver in an old delf jug,
or at their tawdry coloured prints of St. Victorian
or St. Scævola.

But yet much of the beauty and the nobility
of the old, simple, restful rich-hued life of the
past still abode there, and remained with them.
In the straight, lithe form of their maidens, un-
trammelled by modern garb, and moving with

the free majestic grace of forest does. In the vast, dim, sculptured chambers, where the grandam span by the wood fire and the little children played in the shadows, and the lovers whispered in the embrasured window. In the broad market-place, where the mules cropped the clover, and the tawny awnings caught the sunlight, and the white caps of the girls framed faces fitted for the pencils of missal painters, and the flush of colour from mellow wall-fruits and grape-clusters glanced amidst the shelter of deepest freshest green. In the perpetual presence of their cathedral, which through sun and storm, through frost and summer, through noon and midnight stood there amidst them, and watched the galled oxen tread their painful way, and the scourged mules droop their humble heads, and the helpless harmless flocks go forth to the slaughter, and the old weary lives of the men and women pass through hunger and cold to the grave, and the sun and the moon rise and set, and the flowers and the children blossom and fade, and the endless years come and go, bringing peace, bringing war; bringing harvest, bringing famine; bringing life, bringing death; and, beholding these, still said to the multitude in its terrible irony, " Lo ! your God is Love."

This little town lay far from the great Paris highway and all greatly frequented tracks. It was but a short distance from the coast, but near no harbour of greater extent than such as some small fishing village had made in the rocks for the trawlers. Few strangers ever came to it, except some wandering painters or antiquaries. It sent its apples and eggs, its poultry and honey, its colza and corn to the use of the great cities; but it was rarely that any of its own people went thither.

Now and then some one of the oval-faced, blue-eyed, lithe-limbed maidens of its little homely households would sigh and flush and grow restless, and murmur of Paris; and would steal out in the break of a warm grey morning whilst only the birds were still waking; and would patter away in her wooden shoes over the broad, white, southern road, with a stick over her shoulder, and a bundle of all her worldly goods upon the stick. And she would look back often, often, as she went; and when all was lost in the blue haze of distance save the lofty spire which she still saw through her tears, she would say in her heart, with her lips parched and trembling, "I will come back again. I will come back again."

But none such ever did come back.

They came back no more than did the white
sweet sheaves of the lilies which the women
gathered and sent to be bought and sold in the
city—to gleam one faint summer night in a gilded
balcony, and to be flung out the next morning,
withered and dead.

One amongst the few who had thus gone whither
the lilies went, and of whom the people would still
talk as their mules paced homewards through the
lanes at twilight, had been Reine Flamma, the
daughter of the miller of Yprés.

Yprés was a beechen-wooded hamlet on the
northern outskirt of the town, a place of orchards
and wooded tangle; through which there ran a
branch of the brimming river, hastening to seek
and join the sea, and caught a moment on its im-
petuous way, and forced to work by the grim mill-
wheels that had churned the foam-bells there for
centuries. The mill-house was very ancient; its
timbers were carved all over into the semblance
of shields and helmets, and crosses, and fleur-de-
lis, and its frontage was of quaint pargetted
work, black and white, except where the old bla-
zonries had been.

It had been handed down from sire to son
of the same race through many generations—a

race hard, keen, unlearned, superstitious, and caustic-tongued—a race wedded to old ways, credulous of legend, chaste of life, cruel of judgment; harshly strong, yet ignorantly weak; a race holding dearer its heirloom of loveless, joyless, bigoted virtue even than those gold and silver pieces which had ever been its passion, hidden away in earthen pipkins under old apple-roots, or in the crannies of wall timber, or in secret nooks of oaken cupboards.

Claude Flamma, the last of this toilsome, God-fearing, man-begrudging, Norman stock, was true to the type and the traditions of his people.

He was too ignorant even to read; but priests do not deem this a fault. He was avaricious; but many will honour a miser quicker than a spend-thrift. He was cruel; but in the market-place he always took heed to give his mare a full feed, so that if she were pinched of her hay in her stall at home none were the wiser, for she had no language but that of her wistful black eyes; and this is a speech to which men stay but little to listen. The shrewd, old, bitter-tongued, stern-living man was feared and respected with the respect that fear begets; and in truth he had a rigid virtue in his way, and was proud of it, with scorn

for those who found it hard to walk less straightly
and less circumspectly than himself.

He married late ; his wife died in childbirth ; his
daughter grew into the perfection of womanhood
under the cold, hard, narrow rule of his severity and
his superstition. He loved her, indeed, with as much
love as it was possible for him ever to feel, and was
proud of her beyond all other things ; saved for
her, toiled for her, muttered ever that it was for
her when at confession he related how his measures
of flour had been falsely weighted, and how he had
filched from the corn brought by the widow and the
fatherless. For her he had sinned : from one to
whom the good report of his neighbours and the
respect of his own conscience were as the very
breath of life, it was the strongest proof of love
that he could give. But this love never gleamed
one instant in his small sharp grey eyes, nor
escaped ever by a single utterance from his lips.
Reprimand, or homily, or cynical rasping sarcasm, was all she ever heard from him. She believed that he despised, and almost hated her ; he
held it well for women to be tutored in subjection
and in trembling.

At twenty-two Reine Flamma was the most beautiful woman in Calvados, and the most wretched.

She was straight as a pine; cold as snow; graceful as a stem of wheat: lovely and silent; with a mute proud face, in which the eyes alone glowed with a strange, repressed, speechless passion and wishfulness. Her life was simple, pure, chaste, blameless, as the lives of the many women of her race who, before her, had lived and died in the shadow of that water-fed wood had always been. Her father rebuked and girded at her, continually dreaming that he could paint whiter even the spotlessness of this lily, refine even the purity of this virgin gold.

She never answered him anything, nor in anything contradicted his will; not one amongst all the youths and maidens of her birthplace had ever heard so much as a murmur of rebellion from her; and the priests said that such a life as this would be fitter for the cloister than the marriage-bed. None of them ever read the warning that these dark blue slumbering eyes would have given to any who should have had the skill to construe them right. There were none of such skill there; and so she, holding her peace, the men and women noted her ever with a curious dumb reverence, and said amongst themselves that the race of Flamma would die well and nobly in her.

"A saint!" said the good old gentle bishop of the district, as he blessed her one summer evening in her father's house, and rode his mule slowly through the pleasant poplar lanes and breeze-blown fields of colza back to his little quiet homestead, where he tended his own cabbages and garnered his own honey.

Reine Flamma bowed her tall.head meekly, and took his benediction in silence.

The morning after, the miller, rising as his custom was at daybreak, and reciting his paternosters, thanked the Mother of the World that she had given him thus strength and power to rear up his motherless daughter in purity and peace. Then he dressed himself in his grey patched blouse, groped his way down the narrow stair, and went in his daily habit to undraw the bolts and unloose the chains of his dwelling.

There was no need that morning for him; the bolts were already back; the house-door stood wide open; on the threshold a brown hen perched pluming herself; there were the ticking of the clock, the cherming of the birds, the rushing of the water; these were the only sounds upon the silence.

He called his daughter's name: there was no

answer. He mounted to her chamber: it had no
tenant. He searched hither and thither, in the
house, and the stable, and the granary: in the
mill, and the garden, and the wood; he shouted,
he ran, he roused his neighbours, he looked in
every likely and unlikely place: there was no
reply.

There was only the howl of the watch-dog, who
sat with his face to the south and mourned unceasingly.

And from that day neither he nor any man living
there ever heard again of Reine Flamma.

Some indeed did notice that at the same time
there disappeared from the town one who had been
there through all that spring and summer. One
who had lived strangely, and been clad in an odd
rich fashion, and had been whispered as an Eastern
prince by reason of his scattered gold, his unfamiliar tongue, his black-browed, star-eyed, deep-hued,
beauty, like the beauty of the passion-flower. But
none had ever seen this stranger and Reine
Flamma in each other's presence; and the rumour
was discredited as a foulness absurd and unseemly
to be said of a woman whom their bishop had called
a saint. So it died out, breathed only by a few
mouths, and it came to be accepted as a fact that

she must have perished in the deep fast-flowing river by some false step on the mill-timber, as she went at dawn to feed her doves, or by some strange sad trance of sleep-walking, from which she had been known more than once to suffer.

Claudis Flamma said little; it was a wound that bled inwardly. He toiled, and chaffered, and drove hard bargains, and worked early and late with his hireling, and took for the household service an old Norman peasant woman more aged than himself, and told no man that he suffered. All that he ever said was, " She was a saint : God took her ; " and in his martyrdom he found a hard pride and a dull consolation.

It was no mere metaphoric form of words with him. He believed in miracles and all manner of Divine interposition, and he believed likewise that she, his angel, being too pure for earth, had been taken by God's own hand up to the bosom of Mary. This honour which had befallen his first-begotten shed both sanctity and splendour on his cheerless days ; and when the little children and the women saw him pass, they cleared from his way as from a prince's, and crossed themselves as they changed words with one whose daughter was the bride of Christ.

So six years passed away; and the name of Reine Flamma was almost forgotten, but embalmed in memories of religious sanctity, as the dead heart of a saint is embedded in amber and myrrh.

At the close of the sixth year there happened what many said was a thing devil-conceived and wrought out by the devil to the shame of a pure name, and to the hindrance of the people of God.

One winter's night Claudis Flamma was seated in his kitchen, having recently ridden home his mare from the market in the town.

The fire burned in ancient fashion on the hearth, and it was so bitter without that even his parsimonious habits had relaxed, and he had piled some wood, liberally mingled with dry moss, that cracked, and glowed, and shot flame up the wide black shaft of the chimney.

The day's work was over; the old woman-servant sat spinning flax on the other side of the fire ; the great mastiff was stretched sleeping quietly on the brick floor ; the blue pottery, the brass pans, the oaken presses that had been the riches of his race for generations, glimmered in the light ; the doors were barred, the shutters closed ; around the house the winds howled, and beneath its walls the fretting water hissed.

The miller, overcome with the past cold and present warmth, nodded on his wooden settle and slept, and muttered dreamily in his sleep, "A saint—a saint!—God took her."

The old woman, hearing, looked across at him, and shook her head, and went on with her spinning with lips that moved inaudibly: she had been wont to say, out of her taskmaster's hearing, that no woman who was beautiful ever was a saint as well. And some thought that this old creature, Marie Pitchou, who had used to live in a miserable hut on the other side of the wood, had known more than she had chosen to tell of the true fate of Reine Flamma.

Suddenly a blow on the panels of the door sounded through the silence. The miller, awakened in a moment, started to his feet and grasped his ash staff with one hand, and with the other the oil-lamp burning on the tressel. The watch-dog arose, but made no hostile sound.

A step crushed the dead leaves without and passed away faintly; there was stillness again; the mastiff went to the bolted door, smelt beneath it, and scratched at the panels.

On the silence there sounded a small, timid, feeble beating on the wood from without; such a slight fluttering noise as a wounded bird might make in striving to rise.

ʼ "It is nothing evil," muttered Flamma. "If it were evil the beast would not want to have the door opened. It may be some one sick or stray."

All this time he was in a manner charitable, often conquering the niggardly instincts of his character to try and save his soul by serving the wretched. He was a miser, and he loved to gain, and loathed to give; but since his daughter had been taken to the saints he had striven with all his might to do good enough to be taken likewise to that heavenly rest.

Any crust bestowed on the starveling, any bed of straw afforded to the tramp, caused him a sharp pang; but since his daughter had been taken he had tried to please God by this mortification of his own avarice and diminution of his own gains. He could not vanquish the nature that was engrained in him. He would rob the widow of an ephah of wheat, and leave his mare famished in her stall, because it was his nature to find in all such saving a sweet savour; but he would not turn away a beggar or refuse a crust to a wayfarer, lest, thus refusing, he might turn away from him an angel unawares.

The mastiff scratched still at the panels; the sound outside had ceased.

The miller, setting the lamp down on the floor, gripped more firmly the ashen stick, undrew the bolts, turned the stout key, and opened the door slowly, and with caution. A loud gust of wind blew dead leaves against his face; a blinding spray of snow scattered itself over his bent stretching form. In the darkness without, whitened from head to foot, there stood a little child.

The dog went up to her and licked her face with kindly welcome. Claudis Flamma drew her with a rough grasp across the threshold, and went out into the air to find whose footsteps had been those which had trodden heavily away after the first knock.

The snow, however, was falling fast; it was a cloudy moonless night. He did not dare to go many yards from his own portals, lest he should fall into some ambush set by robbers. The mastiff too was quiet, which indicated that there was no danger near, so the old man returned, closed the door carefully, drew the bolts into their places, and came towards the child, whom the woman Pitchou had drawn towards the fire.

She was a child of four or five years old;

huddled in coarse linen and in a little red garment of fox's skin, and blanched from head to
foot, for the flakes were frozen on her and on
the hood that covered, gipsy-like, her curls. It
was a strange, little, ice-cold, ghost-like figure,
but out of this mass of icicles and whiteness there
glowed great beaming frightened eyes and a mouth
like a scarlet berry; the radiance and the contrast of it were like the glow of holly fruit thrust
out from a pile of drifted snow.

The miller shook her by the shoulder.

" Who brought you ? "

" Phratos," answered the child, with a stifled sob
in her throat.

" And who is that ? "

" Phratos," answered the child again.

" Is that a man or a woman ? "

The child made no reply; she seemed not to
comprehend his meaning. The miller shook her
again, and some drops of water fell from the ice
that was dissolving in the warmth.

" Why are you come here ? " he asked, impa-
tiently.

She shook her head, as though to say none knew
so little of herself as she.

" You must have a name," he pursued harshly

and in perplexity. " What are you called ?   Who
are you ? "

The child suddenly raised her great eyes that had
been fastened on the leaping flames, and flashed
them upon his in a terror of bewildered ignorance
—the piteous terror of a stray dog.

" Phratos," she cried once more, and the cry now
was half a sigh, half a shriek.

Something in that regard pierced him and startled
him ; he dropped his hand off her shoulder, and
breathed quickly ; the old woman gave a low cry,
and staring with all her might at the child's small
dark, fierce, lovely face, fell to counting her wooden
beads and mumbling many prayers.

Claudis Flamma turned savagely on her as if
stung by some unseen snake, and willing to wreak
his vengeance on the nearest thing that was at hand.

" Fool ! cease your prating ! " he muttered,
with a brutal oath.   " Take the animal and search
her.   Bring me what you find."

Then he sat down on the stool by the fire, and
braced his lips tightly, and locked his bony hands
upon his knees.   He knew what blow awaited him ;
he was no coward, and he had manhood enough in
him to press any iron into his soul and tell none
that it hurt him.

The old woman drew the stranger aside to a dusky corner of an inner chamber, and began to despoil her of her coverings. The creature did not resist; the freezing cold and long fatigue had numbed and silenced her; her eyelids were heavy with the sleep such cold produces, and she had not strength, because she had not consciousness enough, to oppose whatsoever they might choose to do to her. Only now and then her eyes opened, as they had opened on him, with a sudden lustre and fierceness, like those in a netted animal's impatient but untamed regard.

Pitchou seized and searched her eagerly, stripping her of her warm fox-skin wrap, her scarlet hood of wool, her little rough hempen shirt, which were all dripping with the water from the melted snow.

The skin of the young waif was brown, with a golden bloom on it; it had been tanned by hot suns, but it was soft as silk in texture, and transparent, showing the course of each blue vein. Her limbs were not well nourished, but they were of perfect shape and delicate bone; and the feet were the long, arched, slender feet of the southern side of the Pyrenees.

She allowed herself to be stripped and wrapped

in a coarse piece of homespun linen; she was still half frozen, and in a state of stupor, either from amazement or from fear. She was quite passive, and she never spoke. Her apathy deceived the old crone, who took it for docility, and who, trusting to it, proceeded to take advantage of it, after the manner of her kind. About the small shapely head there hung a band of glittering coins; they were not gold, but the woman Pitchou thought they were, and seized them with gloating hands and ravenous eyes.

The child started from her torpor, shook herself free, and fought to guard them—fiercely, with tooth and nail, as the young fox whose skin she had worn might have fought for its dear life. The old woman on her side strove as resolutely; long curls of the child's hair were clutched out in the struggle; she did not wince or scream, but she fought—fought with all the breath and the blood that were in her tiny body.

She was no match, with all her ferocity and fury, for the sinewy grip of the old peasant; and the coins were torn off her forehead and hidden away in a hole in the wood, out of her sight, where the old peasant hoarded all her precious treasures of copper coins and other trifles that she managed to secrete from her master's all-seeing eyes.

They were little metal sequins engraved with Arabic characters, chained together after the Eastern fashion. To Pitchou they looked a diadem of gold worthy of an empress.

The child watched them thus removed in perfect silence ; from the moment they had been wrenched away, and the battle had been finally lost to her, she had ceased to struggle, as though disdainful of a fruitless contest. But a great hate gathered in her eyes, and smouldered there like a half-stifled fire—it burned on and on for many a long year afterwards, unquenched.

When Pitchou brought her a cup of water and a roll of bread, she would neither eat nor drink, but turned her face to the wall,—mute.

" Those are just her father's eyes," the old woman muttered. She had seen them burn in the gloom of the evening through the orchard trees, as the stars had risen, and Reine Flamma listened to the voice that wooed her to her destruction.

She let the child be, and searched her soaked garments for any written word or any token that might be on them. Fastened roughly to the fox's skin there was a faded letter. Pitchou could not read ; she took it to her master.

Claudis Flamma grasped the paper and turned its superscription to the light of the lamp.

He could not read, but yet at sight of the characters his tough frame trembled, and his withered skin grew red with a sickly, feverish quickening of the blood.

He knew them.

Once, in a time long dead, he had been proud of those slender letters that had been so far more legible than any that the women of her class could pen, and on beholding which the good bishop had smiled, and passed a pleasant word concerning her being almost fitted to be his own clerk and scribe.

For a moment, watching those written cyphers that had no tongue for him, and yet seemed to tell their tale so that they scorched and withered up all the fair honour and pious peace of his old age, a sudden faintness, a sudden swooning sense seized him for the first time in all his life ; his limbs failed him, he sank down on his seat again, he gasped for breath ; he needed not to be told anything, he knew all. He knew that the creature whom he had believed so pure that God had deemed the earth unworthy of her youth was——

his throat rattled, his lips were covered with foam, his ears were filled with a rushing, hollow sound, like the roaring of his own mill-waters in a time of storm.

All at once he started to his feet, and glared at the empty space of the dim chamber, and struck his hands wildly together in the air, and cried aloud:

"She was a saint, I said—a saint! A saint in body and soul! And I thought that God begrudged her, and held her too pure for man!"

And he laughed aloud—thrice.

The child hearing, and heavy with sleep, and eagerly desiring warmth, as a little frozen beast that coils itself in snow to slumber into death, startled by that horrible mirth, came forward.

The shirt fell off her as she moved. Her little naked limbs glimmered like gold in the dusky light; her hair was as a cloud behind her; her little scarlet mouth was half open, like the mouth of a child seeking its mother's kiss; her great eyes, dazzled by the flame, flashed and burned and shone like stars. They had seen the same face ere then in Calvados.

She came straight to Claudis Flamma as though drawn by that awful and discordant laughter, and by that leaping ruddy flame upon the hearth, and she stretched out her arms and murmured a word and smiled, a little dreamily, seeking to sleep, asking to be caressed, desiring she knew not what.

He clenched his fist, and struck her to the ground. She fell without a sound. The blood flowed from her mouth.

He looked at her where she lay, and laughed once more.

" She was a saint!—a saint! And the devil begot in her *that !* "

Then he went out across the threshold and into the night, with the letter still clenched in his hand.

The snow fell, the storm raged, the earth was covered with ice and water; he took no heed, but passed through it, his head bare and his eyes blind.

The dog let him go forth alone, and waited by the child.

CHAPTER III.

ALL night long he was absent.

The old serving woman, terrified, in so far as her dull brutish nature could be roused to fear, did what she knew, what she dared. She raised the little wounded naked creature, and carried her to her own pallet bed; restored her to consciousness by such rude means as she had knowledge of, and staunched the flow of blood.

She did all this harshly, as it was her custom to do all things, and without tenderness or even pity, for the sight of this stranger was unwelcome to her, and she also had guessed the message of that unread letter.

The child had been stunned by the blow, and she had lost some blood, and was weakened and stupified and dazed; yet there seemed to her rough nurse no peril for her life, and by degrees she fell into a feverish, tossing slumber, sobbing sometimes in her sleep, and crying perpetually on the unknown name of Phratos.

The old woman Pitchou stood and looked at her. She who had always known the true story of that disappearance which some had called death and some had deemed a divine interposition, had seen before that transparent brown skin, those hues in cheeks and lips like the carnation leaves, that rich, sun-fed, dusky beauty, those straight dark brows.

"She is his sure enough," she muttered. "He was the first with Reine Flamma. I wonder has he been the last."

And she went down the stairs chuckling, as the low human brute will at any evil thought.

The mastiff stayed beside the child.

She went to the fire and threw more wood on, and sat down again to her spinning-wheel, and span and dozed, and span and dozed again.

She was not curious : to her, possessing that thread to the secret of the past, which her master and her townfolk had never held, it all seemed natural. It was an old, old story ; there had been thousands like it ; it was only strange because Reine Flamma had been held a saint.

The hours passed on ; the lamp paled, and its

flame at last died out ; in the loft above, where the
dog watched, there was no sound ; the old woman
slumbered undisturbed, unless some falling ember
of the wood aroused her.

She was not curious, nor did she care how the
child fared. She had led that deadening life of
perpetual labour and of perpetual want in which the
human animal becomes either a machine or a devil.
She was a machine ; put to what use she might be
—to spin flax, to card wool, to wring a pigeon's
throat, to bleed a calf to death, to bake or stew, to
mumble a prayer or drown a kitten, it was all one
to her. If she had a preference, it might be for the
office that hurt some living thing ; but she did not
care : all she heeded was whether she had pottage
enough to eat at noonday, and the leaden effigy of
her Mary safe round her throat at night.

The night went on, and passed away ; one gleam
of dawn shone through a round hole in the shutter ;
she wakened with a start to find the sun arisen, and
the fire dead upon the hearth.

She shook herself and stamped her chill feet
upon the bricks, and tottered on her feeble way,
with frozen body, to the house door. She drew
it slowly open, and saw by the light of the sun that
it had been for some time morning.

The earth was everywhere thick with snow; a hoar frost sparkled over all the branches; great sheets of ice were whirled down the rapid mill-stream; in one of the leafless boughs a robin sang, and beneath the bough a cat was crouched, waiting with hungry eager eyes, patient even in its famished impatience.

Dull as her sympathy was, and slow her mind, she started as she saw her master there.

Claudis Flamma was at work; the rough, hard, rude toil, which he spared to himself no more than to those who were his hirelings. He was carting wood; going to and fro with huge limbs of trees that men in youth would have found it a severe task to move; he was labouring breathlessly, giving himself no pause, and the sweat was on his brow, although he trod ankle deep in snow, and although his clothes were heavy with icicles.

He did not see or hear her; she went up to him and called him by his name; he started, and raised his head and looked at her.

Dull though she was, she was in a manner frightened by the change upon his face; it had been lean, furrowed, weather-beaten always, but it was livid now, with bloodshot eyes, and a bruised, broken, yet withal savage look that

E 2

terrified her. He did not speak, but gazed at her like a man recalled from some drugged sleep back to the deeds and memories of the living world.

The old woman held her peace a few moments; then spoke out in her own blunt, dogged fashion.

" Is she to stay ? "

Her mind was not awake enough for any curiosity; she only cared to know if the child stayed : only so much as would concern her soup kettle, her kneaded dough, her spun hemp, her household labour.

He turned for a second with the gesture that a trapped fox may make, held fast, yet striving to essay a death grip; then he checked himself, and gave a mute sign of assent, and heaved up a fresh log of wood, and went on with his labours, silently. She knew of old his ways too well to venture to ask more. She knew, too, that when he worked like this, fasting and in silence, there had been long and fierce warfare in his soul, and some great evil done for which he sought to make atonement.

So she left him, and passed in to the house, and built up afresh her fire, and swept her chamber out, and fastened up her round black pot to boil, and muttered all the while,—

"Another mouth to feed; another beast to tend."

And the thing was bitter to her; because it gave trouble and took food.

Now, what the letter had been, or who had deciphered it for him, Claudis Flamma never told to any man; and from the little strange creature no utterance could be ever got.

But the child who had come in the night and the snow tarried at Yprès from that time thenceforward.

Claudis Flamma nourished, sheltered, clothed her; but he did all these begrudgingly, harshly, scantily; and he did all these with an acrid hate and scorn, which did not cease but rather grew with time.

The blow which had been her earliest welcome was not the first that she received from him by many; and whilst she was miserable exceedingly, she showed it, not as children do, but rather like some chained and untamed animal, in tearless stupor and in sudden, sharp ferocity. And this the more because she spoke but a very few words of the language of the people amongst whom she had been brought; her own tongue was one full of round vowels and strange sounds, a tongue unknown to them.

For many weeks he said not one word to her, cast not one look at her ; he let her lead the same life that was led by the beetles that crawled in the timbers, or by the pigs that couched and were kicked in the straw. The woman Pitchou gave her such poor scraps of garments or of victuals as she chose ; she could crouch in the corner of the hearth where the fire warmth reached ; she could sleep in the hay in the little loft under the roof ; so much she could do and no more.

After that first moment in which her vague appeal for pity and for rest had been answered by the blow that struck her senseless, the child had never made a moan, nor sought for any solace.

All the winter through she lay curled up on the tiles by the fence, with her arms round the great body of the dog and his head upon her chest ; they were both starved, beaten, kicked, and scourged, with brutal words oftentimes ; they had the community of misfortune, and they loved one another.

The blow on her head, the coldness of the season, the scanty food that was cast to her, all united to keep her brain stupified and her body almost motionless. She was like a young bear that is motherless, wounded, frozen, famished, but which, coiled in an almost continual slumber, keeps its blood flowing and its limbs alive. And, like the bear, with the spring she awakened.

When the townsfolk and the peasants came to the mill, and first saw this creature there, with her wondrous vivid hues, and her bronzed half-naked limbs, they regarded her in amazement, and asked the miller whence she came. He set his teeth, and answered ever :

" The woman that bore her was Reine Flamma."

The avowal was a penance set to himself, but to it he never added more ; and they feared his bitter temper and his caustic tongue too greatly to press it on him, or even to ask him whether his daughter were with the living or the dead.

With the unfolding of the young leaves, and the loosening of the frost-bound waters, and the unveiling of the violet and the primrose under the shadows of the wood, all budding life revives, and so did hers. For she could escape from the dead, cold, bitter atmosphere of the silent and loveless house, where her bread was begrudged, and the cudgel was her teacher, out into the freshness and the living sunshine of the young blossoming world, where the birds and the beasts and the tender blue flowers and the curling green boughs were her comrades, and where she could stretch her limbs in freedom, and coil herself among the branches, and steep her limbs in the coolness of waters, and bathe her aching feet in the moisture of rain-filled grasses.

With the spring she arose, the true forest animal she was; wild, fleet, incapable of fear, sure of foot, in unison with all the things of the earth and the air, and stirred by them to a strange, dumb, ignorant, passionate gladness.

She had been scarce seen in the winter; with the breaking of the year the people from more distant places, who rode their mules down to the mill on their various errands, stared at this child and wondered amongst themselves greatly, and at length asked Claudis Flamma whence she came.

He answered ever, setting hard his teeth:

"The woman that bore her was one accursed, whom men deemed a saint—Reine Flamma."

They dared not ask him more; for many were his debtors.

But when they went away, and gossiped amongst themselves by the wayside well or under the awnings of the market stalls, they said to one another that it was just as they had thought long ago; the creature had been no better than her kind ; and they had never credited the fable that God had taken her, though they had humoured the miller because he was aged and in his dotage. Whilst one old woman, a withered and witch-like crone, who had toiled in from the fishing village with a kreel upon her back and the smell of the sea about her rags, heard, standing in the market-place, and laughed, and mocked them, these seers who were so wise after the years had gone, and when the truth was clear.

"You knew, you knew, you knew!" she echoed, with a grin upon her face. "Oh, yes! you were so wise! Who, seven years through, said that Reine Flamma was a saint, and taken by the saints into their keeping? And who hissed at me for a foul-mouthed crone when I said that the devil had more to do with her than the good God, and that the black-browed gipsy, with jewels for eyes in his head, like the toad, was the only master to whom she gave herself? Oh-hé, you were so wise!"

So she mocked them, and they were ashamed, and held their peace ; well knowing that indeed no creature amongst them had ever been esteemed so pure, so chaste, and so honoured of heaven as had been the miller's daughter.

Many remembered the "gipsy with the jewelled eyes," and saw those brilliant, fathomless, midnight eyes reproduced in the small rich face of the child whom Reine Flamma, as her own father said, had borne in shame whilst they had been glorifying her apotheosis. And it came to be said, as time went on, that this unknown stranger had been the fiend himself, taking human shape for the destruction of one pure soul, and the confusion of all true children of the church.

Legend and tradition still held fast their minds in this remote, ancient, and priest-ridden place ; in their belief the devil was still a living power, traversing the earth and air in search of souls, and not seldom triumphing: of metaphor or myth they were ignorant, Satan to them was a personality, terrific, and oftentimes irresistible, assuming at will shapes grotesque or awful, human or spiritual. Their forefathers had beheld him ; why not they ?

So the henhucksters and poulterers, the cider-makers and tanners, the fisherfolk from the sea-board, and the peasant proprietors from the country round, came at length in all seriousness to regard the young child at Yprès as a devil-born thing. "She was hell-begotten," they would mutter, when they saw her; and they would cross themselves, and avoid her if they could.

The time had gone by, unhappily, as they considered, when men had been permitted to burn such creatures as this; they knew it and were sorry for it; the world, they thought, had been better when Jews had blazed like torches, and witches had crackled like firewood; such treats were forbidden now, they knew, but many, for all that, thought within themselves that it was a pity it should be so, and that it was mistaken mercy in the age they lived in which forbade the purifying of the earth by fire of such as she.

In the winter time, when they first saw her, unusual floods swept the country, and destroyed much of their property; in the spring which followed there were mildew and sickness everywhere; in the summer there was a long drought, and by consequence there came a bad harvest, and great suffering and scarcity.

There were not a few in the district who attributed all these woes to the advent of the child of darkness, and who murmured openly in their huts and homesteads that no good would befall them so long as this offspring of hell were suffered in their midst.

Since, however, the time was past when the broad market place could have been filled with a curious, breathless, eager crowd, and the grey cathedral have grown red in the glare of flames fed by a young living body, they held their hands from doing her harm, and said these things only in their own ingle-nooks, and contented themselves with forbidding their children to consort with her, and with drawing their mules to the other side of the road when they met her. They did not mean to be cruel, they only acted in their own self-defence, and dealt with her as their fellow countrymen dealt with a cagote—"only."

Hence, when, with the reviving year the child's dulled brain awakened, and all the animal activity in her sprang into vigorous action, she found herself shunned, marked, and glanced at with averted looks of mingled dread and scorn. "A daughter of the devil!" she heard again and again muttered as they passed her; she grew to take shelter in this repute as in a fortress, and to be proud, with a savage pride, of her imputed origin.

It made her a little fierce, mute, fearless, reckless, all daring, and all enduring animal. An animal in her ferocities, her mute instincts, her supreme patience, her physical perfectness of body and of health. Perfect of shape and hue; full of force to resist; ignorant either of hope or fear; desiring only one thing, liberty; with no knowledge, but with unerring instinct.

She was at an age when happier creatures have scarce escaped from their mother's arms; but she had not even thus early a memory of her mother, and she had been shaken off to live or die, to fight or famish, as a young fox whose dam has been flung to the hounds is driven away to starve in the winter woods, or save himself, if he have strength, by slaughter.

She was a tame animal only in one thing:—she took blows uncomplainingly, and as though comprehending that they were her inevitable portion.

"The child of the devil!" they said. In a dumb, half unconscious fashion, this five-year-old creature wondered sometimes why the devil had not been good enough to give her a skin that would not feel, and veins that would not bleed.

She had always been beaten ever since her birth; she was beaten here; she thought it a law of life as other children think it such to have their mother's kiss and their daily food and nightly prayer.

Claudis Flamma did after his manner his duty by her. She was to him a thing accursed, possessed, loathsome, imbued with evil from her origin; but he did what he deemed his duty. He clothed her, if scantily; he fed her, if meagrely; he lashed her with all the caustic gibes that came naturally to his tongue; he set her hard tasks to keep her from idleness; he beat her when she did not, and not seldom when she did, them. He dashed holy water on her many times; and used a stick to her without mercy.

After this light he did his duty. That he should hate her, was to fulfil a duty also in his eyes; he had always been told that it was right to abhor the things of darkness; and to him she was a thing of utter darkness, a thing born of the black ruin of a stainless soul, begotten by the pollution and corruption of an infernal tempter.

He never questioned her as to her past—that short past, like the span of an insect's life, which yet had sufficed to gift her with passions, with instincts, with desires, even with memories,—in a word, with character :—a character he could neither change nor break; a thing formed already, for good or for evil, abidingly.

He never spoke to her except in sharp irony

or in curt command. He set her hard tasks of bodily labour which she did not dispute, but accomplished so far as her small strength lay, with a mute dogged patience, half ferocity, half passiveness.

In those first winter days of her arrival he called her Folle-Farine ; taking the most worthless, the most useless, the most abject, the most despised thing he knew in all his daily life from which to name her ; and the name adhered to her, and was the only one by which she was ever known.

Folle-Farine !—as one may say, the Dust.

In time she grew to believe that it was really hers ; even as in time she began to forget that strange, deep, rich tongue in which she had babbled her first words, and to know no other tongue than the Norman-French about her.

Yet in her there existed imagination, tenderness, gratitude, and a certain wild and true nobility, though the old man Flamma would never have looked for them, never have believed in them. She was devil-born : she was of devil nature in his eyes.

Upon his mill-ditch, foul and fœtid, refuse would sometimes gather, and receiving the seed of the lily, would give birth to blossoms born stainless

out of corruption : but the allegory had no meaning for him.　Had any one pointed it out to him he
would have taken the speaker into his orchard, and
said :

"Will the crab bear a fruit not bitter? Will the
nightshade give out sweetness and honey? Fool!
—as the stem so the branch, as the sap so the
blossom."

And this fruit of sin and shame was poison in
his sight.

CHAPTER IV.

THE little dim mind of the five-year-old child was not a blank; it was indeed filled to overflowing with pictures of a country that her tongue could not have told of, even had she spoken the language of the people amidst whom she had been cast.

A land altogether unlike that in which she had been set down on that bitter night of snow and storm: a land noble and wild, and full of colour, broken into vast heights and narrow valleys, clothed with green beechwoods and with forests of oak and of walnut, filled with the noise of torrents leaping from crag to crag, and of brown mountain streams rushing, broad and angry, through wooded ravines. A land made beautiful by moss-grown water-mills, and lofty gateways of grey rock; and still shadowy pools, in which the bright fish leaped; and mules' bells that rang drowsily through leafy gorges; and limestone crags that pierced the clouds, spire-like, and fantastic in a thousand shapes; and high blue crests of snow-topped mountains, whose pinnacles glowed to the divinest flush of rose and amber with the setting of the sun.

This land she remembered vaguely, yet gloriously, as the splendours of a dream of Paradise rest on the brain of some young sleeper wakening in squalor, cold, and pain. But the people of the place she had been brought to could not comprehend her few, shy, sullen words, and her strange imperfect trills of song; and she could not tell them that this land had been no realm enchanted of fairy or of fiend, but only the forest region of the Liébana.

Thither, one rich autumn day, a tribe of Spanish gypsies had made their camp. They were a score in all; they held themselves one of the noblest branches of their wide family; they were people with pure Eastern blood in them, and all the grace and the gravity of the Oriental in their forms and postures.

They stole horses and sheep; they harried cattle; they stopped the mules in the passes, and lightened their load of wine-skins: they entered the posada, when they deigned to enter one at all, with neither civil question nor show of purse, but with a gleam of the teeth, like a threatening dog, and the flash of the knife, half drawn out of the girdle. They were low thieves and mean liars; wild daredevils and loose livers; loathers of labour and lovers of idle days and plundering nights; yet they were beautiful, with the noble, calm, scornful beauty of the East, and they wore their rags with an air that was in itself an empire.

They could play, too, in heavenly fashion, on their old three-stringed viols; and when their women danced on the sward by moonlight, under the broken shadows of some Moorish ruin, clanging high their tambourines above their graceful heads, and tossing the shining sequins that bound their heavy hair, the muleteer or the herdsman, seeing them from afar, shook with fear, and thought of the tales told him in his childhood by his grandam of the spirits of the dead Moors that rose to revelry, at midnight, in the haunts of their old lost kingdom.

Amongst them was a man yet more handsome than the rest, taller and lither still; wondrous at leaping and wrestling, and all athletic things; surest of any to win a woman, to tame a horse, to

strike down a bull at a blow, to silence an angry
group at a wineshop with a single glance of his
terrible eyes.

His name was Taric.

He had left them often to wander by himself into
many countries, and at times when, by talent or by
terrorism, he had netted gold enough to play the
fool to his fancy, he had gone to some strange city,
where credulity and luxury prevailed, and there had
lived like a prince, as his own phrase ran, and
gamed and intrigued, and feasted, and roystered
right royally whilst his gains lasted.

Those spent, he would always return awhile,
and lead the common, roving, thieving life of
his friends and brethren, till the fit of ambition
or the run of luck were again on him. Then
his people would afresh lose sight of him to light
on him, velvet-clad, and wine-bibbing, in some
painter's den in some foreign town, or welcome him
ragged, famished, and footweary, on their own sunburnt sierras.

And the mystery of his ways endeared him
to them; and they made him welcome whenever he returned, and never quarrelled with him
for his faithlessness; but if there were anything
wilder or wickeder, bolder or keener, on hand

than was usual, his tribe would always say—"Let Taric lead."

One day their camp was made in a gorge under the great shadows of the Picos da Europa, a place that they loved much, and settled in often, finding the chesnut woods and the cliff caverns fair for shelter, the heather abounding in grouse, and the pools full of trout, fair for feeding. That day Taric returned from a year-long absence, suddenly standing, dark and mighty, between them and the light, as they lay around their soup kettle, awaiting their evening meal.

" There is a woman in labour, a league back; by the great cork-tree, against the bridge," he said to them. " Go to her some of you."

And, with a look to the women which singled out two for the errand, he stretched himself in the warmth of the fire, and helped himself to the soup, and lay quiet, vouchsafing them never a word, but playing meaningly with the knife handle thrust into his shirt; for he saw that some of the men were about to oppose his share of a common meal which he had not earned by a common right.

It was Taric—a name of some terror came to their fierce souls.

Taric, the strongest and fleetest and most well-

favoured of them all; Taric, who had slain the
bull that all the matadors had failed to daunt;
Taric, who had torn up the young elm, when
they needed a bridge over a flood, as easily as
a child plucks up a reed; Taric, who had stopped
the fiercest contrabandista in all those parts, and
cut the man's throat with no more ado than a
butcher slits a lamb's.

So they were silent, and let him take his portion
of the fire and of the broth, and of the thin red
wine.

Meanwhile the two gypsies, Quità and Zarâ,
went on their quest, and found things as he had
said.

Under the great cork-tree, where the grass
was long and damp, and the wood grew thickly,
and an old rude bridge of unhewn blocks of rock
spanned, with one arch, the river as it rushed
downward from its limestone bed aloft, they found
a woman just dead, and a child just born.

Quità looked the woman all over hastily, to see if,
by any chance, any gold or jewels might be on her;
there were none. There was only an ivory cross on
her chest, which Quità drew off and hid. Quità
covered her with a few boughs and left her.

Zarâ wrapped the child in a bit of her woollen

skirt, and held it warm in her breast, and hastened
to the camp with it.

" She is dead, Taric," said Quità, meaning the
woman she had left.

He nodded his handsome head.

" This is yours, Taric ? " said Zarâ, meaning the
child she held.

He nodded again, and drank another drop of
wine, and stretched himself.

" What shall we do with her ? " asked Quità.

" Let her lie there," he answered her.

" What shall we do with it ? " asked Zarâ.

He laughed, and drew his knife against his own
brown throat in a significant gesture.

Zarâ said no word to him, but she went away
with the child under some branches, on which was
hung a tattered piece of awning, orange striped,
that marked her own especial resting place.

Out of the group about the fire, one man, rising,
advanced, and looked Taric full in the eyes.

" Has the woman died by foul means ? "

Taric, who never let any living soul molest or
menace him, answered him without offence, and
with a savage candour.

" No—that I swear. I used no foul play against
her. Go look at her if you like. I loved her well

enough while she lived. But what does that matter?
She is dead. So best. Women are as many as the
mulberries."

"You loved her, and you will let the wolves eat
her body?"

Taric laughed.

"There are few wolves in the Liébana. Go and
bury her if you choose, Phratos."

"I will," the other answered him; and he took
his way to the cork-tree by the bridge.

The man who spoke was called Phratos.

He was not like his tribe in anything: except in
a mutual love for a life that wandered always, and
was to no man responsible, and needed no roof-tree,
and wanted no settled habitation, but preferred to
dwell wild with the roe and the coney, and to be
hungry and unclad, rather than to eat the good
things of the earth in submission and in durance.

He had not their physical perfection: an accident
at his birth had made his spine misshapen, and his
gait halting. His features would have been grotesque in their ugliness, except for the sweet pathos
of the eyes and the gay archness of the mouth.

Amongst a race noted for its singular beauty of face
and form, Phratos alone was deformed and unlovely;
and yet both deformity and unloveliness were in a

way poetic and uncommon; and in his rough sheepskin garments, knotted to his waist with a leathern
thong, and with his thick tangled hair falling down on
his shoulders, they were rather the deformity of the
brake-haunting faun, the unloveliness of the moon-
dancing satyr, than those of a man and a vagrant.
With the likeness he had the temper of the old
dead gods of the forests and rivers ; he loved music,
and could make it, in all its innumerable sighs and
songs, give a voice to all creatures and things of the
world, of the waters and the woodlands ; and for
many things he was sorrowful continually, and for
other things he for ever laughed and was glad.

Though he was misshapen, and even, as some
said, not altogether straight in his wits, yet his kin
honoured him.

For he could draw music from the rude strings
of his old viol that surpassed their own melodies
as far as the shining of the sun on the summits
of the Europa surpassed the trembling of the little
lamps under the painted road-side Calvaries.

He was only a gypsy; he only played as the fancy
moved him, by a bright fountain at a noonday halt,
under the ruined arches of a Saracenic temple ;
before the tawny gleam of a vast dim plain at sunrise ; in a cool shadowy court, where the vines shut

out all light; beneath a balcony at night, when the moonbeams gleamed on some fair unknown face, thrust for a moment from the darkness through the white magnolia flowers. Yet he played in suchwise as makes women weep, and holds children and dogs still to listen, and moves grown men to shade their eyes with their hands, and think of old dead times, when they played and prayed at their mothers' knees. .

And his music had so spoken to himself that, although true to his tribe and all their traditions, loving the vagrant life in the open air, and being incapable of pursuing any other, he yet neither stole nor slew, neither tricked nor lied, but found his way vaguely to honesty and candour, and, having found them, clove to them, so that none could turn him: living on such scant gains as were thrown to him for his music from balconies and posada windows and winehouse doors in the hamlets and towns through which he passed, and making a handful of pulse and a slice of melon, a couch of leaves and a draught of water, suffice to him for his few and simple wants.

His people reproached him, indeed, with demeaning their race by taking payment in lieu of making thefts; and they mocked him often,

and taunted him, though in a manner they all
loved him,—the reckless and bloodstained Taric
most, perhaps, of all. But he would never
quarrel with them, neither would he give over his
strange ways which so incensed them, and with time
they saw that Phratos was a gifted fool, who, like
other mad simple creatures, had best be left to
go on his own way unmolested and without con-
tradiction.

If, too, they had driven him from their midst,
they would have missed his music sorely; that
music which awoke them at break of day soaring up
through their roof of chesnut leaves like a lark's
song piercing the skies.

Phratos came now to the dead woman, and
drew off the boughs, and looked at her. She was
quite dead. She had died where she had first sunk
down, unable to reach her promised resting place.
It was a damp green nook on the edge of the
bright mountain river, at the entrance of that
narrow gorge in which the encampment had been
made.

The face, which was white and young, lay upward, with the shadows of the flickering foliage
on it; and the eyes, which Quità had not
closed, were large and blue; her hair, which was

long and brown, was loose, and had got wet amongst the grass, and had little buds of flowers and stray golden leaves twisted in it.

Phratos felt sorrow for her as he looked.

He could imagine her history.

Taric, whom many women had loved, had besought many a one thus to share his fierce free life for a little space, and then drift away out of it by chance, or be driven away from it by his fickle passions, or be taken away like this woman by death.

In her bosom, slipped in her clothes, was a letter. It was written in a tongue he did not know. He held it awhile, thinking, then he folded it up and put it in his girdle,—it might be of use, who could tell? There was the child, there, that might live; unless the camp broke up, and Zarâ left it under a walnut tree to die, with the last butterflies of the fading summer, which was in all likelihood all she would do.

Nevertheless he kept the letter, and when he had looked long enough at the dead creature, he turned to the tools he had brought with him, and set patiently to make her grave.

He could only work slowly, for he was weak of body, and his infirmity made all manual toil painful

to him.   His task was hard, even though the earth
was so soft from recent heavy rains.

The sun set whilst he was still engaged on
it; and it was quite nightfall before he had
fully accomplished it.   When the grave was
ready he filled it carefully with the golden leaves
that had fallen, and the thick many-coloured
mosses that covered the ground like a carpet.

Then he laid the body tenderly down within that
forest shroud, and, with the moss like a winding-
sheet between it and the earth which had to fall
on it, he committed the dead woman to her resting-
place.

It did not seem strange to him, or awful, to leave
her there.

He was a gypsy, and to him a grave under a
forest tree and by a mountain stream seemed
the most natural rest at last that any creature
could desire or claim.   No rites seemed needful to
him, and no sense of any neglect, cruel or un-
fitting, jarred on him in thus leaving her in her
loneliness, with only the cry of the bittern or the
bell of the wild roe as a requiem.

Yet a certain sorrow for this unknown and
lost life was on him, bohemian though he was,
as he took up his mattock and turned away,

and went backward down the gorge, and left
her to lie there for ever, through rain and sunshine, through wind and storm, through the
calm of the summer and the flush of the autumn,
and the wildness of the winter, when the swollen
stream should sweep above her tomb, and the
famished beasts of the hills would lift up their
voices around it.

When he reached the camp, he gave the letter to
Taric.

Taric, knowing the tongue it was written in, and
being able to understand the character, looked at
it, and read it through by the light of the flaming
wood. When he had done so he tossed it behind,
in among the boughs, in scorn.

"The poor fool's prayer to the brute that she
hated !" he said, with a scoff.

Phratos lifted up the letter and kept it.

In a later time he found some one who could
decipher it for him.

It was the letter of Reine Flamma to the miller
at Yprès, telling him the brief story of her fatal
passion, and imploring from him mercy to her
unborn child should it survive her and be ever
taken to him.

Remorse and absence had softened to her the

harshness and the meanness of her father's character; she only remembered that he had loved
her, and had deemed her pure and faithful as the
saints of God. There was no word in the appeal
by which it could have been inferred that Claudis
Flamma had been other than a man much wronged
and loving much, patient of heart, and without
blame in his simple life.

Phratos took the letter and cherished it. He
thought it might some day serve her offspring.
This old man's vengeance could not, he thought,
be so cruel to the child as might be the curse and
the knife of Taric.

"She must have been beautiful?" said Phratos
to him, after a while, that night; "and you care
no more for her than that."

Taric stretched his mighty limbs in the warmth
of the flame and made his answer:

"There will be as good grapes on the vines next
year as any we gathered this. What does it sig-
nify?—she was only a woman.

"She loved me; she thought me a god, a
devil, a prince, a chief,—all manner of things;—
the people thought so too. She was sick of
her life. She was sick of the priests and the
beads, and the mill and the market. She was fair

to look at, and the fools called her a saint. When a woman is young and has beauty, it is dull to be worshipped—in that way.

"I met her in the wood one summer night. The sun was setting. I do not know why I cared for her—I did. She was like a tall white lily; these women of ours are only great tawny sunflowers.

"She was pure and straight of life; she believed in heaven and hell; she was innocent as a child unborn; it was tempting to kill all that. It is so easy to kill it when a woman loves you. I taught her what passion and freedom and pleasure and torment all meant. She came with me,—after a struggle, a hard one. I kept her loyally while the gold lasted; that I swear. I took her to many cities. I let her have jewels and music, and silk dresses, and fine linen. I was good to her; that I swear.

"But after a bit she pined, and grew dull again, and wept in secret, and at times I caught her praying to the white cross which she wore on her breast. That made me mad. I cursed her and beat her. She never said anything; she seemed only to love me more, and that made me more mad.

"Then I got poor again, and I had to sell her things one by one. Not that she minded that, she would have sold her soul for me. We wandered north and south; and I made money sometimes by the dice, or by breaking a horse, or by fooling a woman, or by snatching a jewel off one of their dolls in their churches; and I wanted to get rid of her, and I could not tell how. I had not the heart to kill her outright.

"But she never said a rough word, you know, and that makes a man mad. Maddalena or Kara or Rachel—any of them,—would have flown and struck a knife at me, and hissed like a snake, and there would have been blows and furious words and bloodshed; and then we should [have kissed, and been lovers again, fast and fierce. But a woman who is quiet, and only looks at you with great, sad, soft eyes, when you strike her,—what is one to do?

"We were horribly poor at last: we slept in barns and haylofts; we ate berries and drank the brook water. She grew weak, and could hardly walk. Many a time I have been tempted to let [her lie and die in the hedgeway or on the plains, and I did not,—one is so foolish sometimes for sake of a woman. She knew she

was a burden and, curse to me,—I may have said
so, perhaps; I do not remember.

"At last I heard of you in the Liébana, from
a tribe we fell in with on the other side of the
mountains, and so we travelled here on foot.   I
thought she would have got to the women before
her hour arrived.   But she fell down there, and
could not. stir: and so the end came. It is
best as it is.   She was wretched, and what
could I do with a woman like that, who would
never hearken to another lover, nor give up her
dead God on his cross, nor take so much as a broken
crust if it were stolen, nor even show her beauty to
a sculptor to be carved in stone—for I tried to
make her do that, and she would not.   It is best as
it is.   If she had lived we could have done nothing
with her.   And yet I see her sometimes as I saw
her that night, so white and so calm, in the little
green wood, as the sun set——"

His voice ceased, and he took up a horn full of
vino clarete ; and drained it, and was very still,
stretching his limbs to bask in the heat of the
fire.   The wine had loosened his tongue, and he
had spoken from his heart,—truthfully.

Phratos, his only hearer, was silent.

He was thinking of the great blue sightless eyes

that he had closed, and of the loose brown hair on which he had flung the wet leaves and the earth-clogged mosses.

" The child lives ? " he said at length.

Taric, who was sinking to sleep after the long fatigues of a heavy tramp through mountain passes, stirred sullenly with an oath.

" Let it go to hell," he made answer.

And these were the only words of baptism that were spoken over the nameless daughter of Taric the gypsy and of Reine Flamma.

That night Phratos called out to him in the moonlight the woman Zarâ, who came from under her tent, and stood under the glistening leaves, strong and handsome, with shining eyes and snowy teeth.

" The child lives still ? " he asked.

Zarâ nodded her head.

" You will try and keep it alive ? " he pursued.

She shrugged her shoulders.

" What is the use ? Taric would rather it were dead."

" What matter what Taric wishes. Living or dead, it will not hinder him. A child more or less with us, what is it ? Only a draught of goat's milk or a handful of meal. So little ; it cannot be felt.

You have a child of your own, Zarâ; you cared for it?"

"Yes," she answered, with a sudden softening gleam of her bright savage eyes.

She had a brown, strong, year-old boy, who kicked his naked limbs on the sward with joy at Phratos' music.

"Then have pity on this motherless creature," said Phratos, wooingly. "I buried that dead woman; and her eyes, though there was no sight in them, still seemed to pray to mine—and to pray for her child. Be merciful, Zarâ. Let the child have the warmth of your arms and the defence of your strength. Be merciful, Zarâ; and your seed shall multiply and increase tenfold, and shall be stately and strong, and shall spread as the branches of the plane-trees, on which the storm spends its fury in vain, and beneath which all things of the earth can find refuge. For never was a woman's pity fruitless, nor the fair deeds of her days without recompense."

Zarâ listened quietly, as the dreamy, poetic, persuasive words stole on her ear like music. Like the rest of her people, she half believed in him as a seer and prophet; her teeth shone out in a soft sudden smile.

" You are always a fool, Phratos," she said;
" but it shall be as you fancy."

And she went in out of the moonlit leaves and the
clear cool, autumn night into the little dark stifling
tent, where the new-born child had been laid away
in a corner upon a rough-and-ready bed of gathered
dusky fir-needles.

" It is a little cub, not worth the saving ; and its
dam was not of our people," she said to herself, as
she lifted the wailing and alien creature to her
bosom.

" It is for you, my angel, that I do it," she murmured, looking at the sleeping face of her own son.

Outside the tent the sweet strains of Phratos'
music rose sighing and soft; and mingling, as sounds
mingle in a dream, with the murmurs of the forest
leaves and the rushing of the mountain river. He
gave her the only payment in his power.

Zarâ, hushing the strange child at her breast,
listened, and was half-touched half-angered.

" Why should he play for this little stray thing,
when he never played once for you, my glory ?" she
said to her son, as she put the dead woman's child
roughly away, and took him up in its stead, to beat
together in play his rosy hands and cover his mouth
with kisses.

For even from these, the world's outcasts, this new life of a few hours' span was rejected as unworthy and despised.

Nevertheless, the music played on through the still forest night; and nevertheless, the child grew and throve.

The tribe of Taric abode in the Liébana or in the adjacent country along the banks of the Deva during the space of four years and more, scarcely losing in that time the sight, either from near or far, of the rosy peaks of the Europa.

He did not abide with them; he quarrelled with them violently concerning some division of a capture of wineskins, and went on his own way to distant provinces and cities; to the gambling and the roystering, the woman-fooling and the bull-fighting, that his soul lusted after always.

His daughter he left to dwell in the tent of Zarâ, and under the defence of Phratos.

Once or twice, in sojourns of a night or two amongst his own people, as the young creature grew in stature and strength, Taric had glanced at her, and called her to him, and felt the litheness of her limbs and the weight of her hair, and laughed as he thrust her from him, thinking that, in time to come, she—who would know nothing of her mother's dead

God on the cross, and of her mother's idle, weak scruples,—might bring him a fair provision in his years of age, when his hand should have lost its weight against men and his form its goodliness in the sight of women.

Once or twice he had given her a kick of his foot, or blow with his leathern whip, when she crawled in the grass too near his path, or lay asleep in the sun as he chanced to pass by her.

Otherwise he had nought to do with her, absent or present; otherwise he left her to chance and the devil, who were, as he said, according to the Christians, the natural patrons and sponsors of all love children. Chance and the devil, however, had not wholly their way in the Liébana; for beside them there was Phratos.

Phratos never abandoned her.

Under the wolfskin and pineboughs of Zarâ's tent there was misery very often.

Zarâ had a fresh son born to her with each succeeding year; and having a besotted love for her own offspring, had little but indifference and blows for the stranger who shared their bed and food. Her children, brown and curly, naked and strong, fought one another like panther cubs, and rode in a cluster like red mountain-ash

berries in the sheep-skin round her waist, and
drank by turns out of the pitcher of broth, and
slept all together on dry ferns and mosses, rolled in
warm balls one in another like young bears.

But the child who had no affinity with them, who
was not even wholly of their tribe, but had in her
what they deemed the taint of gentile blood, was
not allowed to gnaw her bare bone or her ripe fig in
peace if they wished for it ; was never carried with
them in the sheep-skin nest, but left to totter after
in the dust or mud as best she might ; was forced
to wait for the leavings in the pitcher, or go without
if leavings there were none ; and was kicked away
by the sturdy limbs of these young males when she
tried to creep for warmth's sake in amongst them
on their fern bed. But she minded all this little ;
since in the Liébana there was Phratos.

Phratos was always good to her. The prayer
which those piteous dead eyes had made he always
answered. He had always pity for the child.

Many a time, but for his remembrance, she would
have starved outright or died of cold in those wild
winters, when the tribe huddled together in the
caverns of the limestone, and the snow-drifts were
driven up by northern winds and blocked them there
for many days. Many a time but for his aid she would

have dropped on their march and been left to perish as she might on the long sunburnt roads, in the arid mid-summers, when the gypsies plodded on their dusty way through the sinuous windings of hill-side paths and along the rough stones of dried-up water courses, in gorges and passages known alone to them and the wild deer.

When her throat was parched with the torment of long thirst, it was he who raised her to drink from the rill in' the rock, high above, to which the mothers lifted their eager children leaving her to gasp and gaze unpitied. When she was driven away from the noonday meal by the hungry and clamorous youngsters, who would admit no share of their partridge broth and stewed lentils, it was he who bruised the maize between stones for her eating, and gathered for her the wild fruit of the quince and the mulberry.

When the sons of Zarâ had kicked and bruised and spurned her from the tent, he would lead her away to some shadowy place where the leaves grew thickly, and play to her such glad and buoyant tunes that the laughter seemed to bubble from the listening brooks and ripple amongst the swinging boughs, and make the wild hare skip with joy, and draw the timid

lizard from his hole to frolic.   And when the way
was long, and the stony paths cruel to her little
bare feet, he would carry her aloft on his
misshapen shoulders, where his old viol always
travelled ; and would beguile the steep way with a
thousand quaint, soft, grotesque conceits of all the
flowers and leaves and birds and animals: talking
rather to himself than her, yet talking with a tender
fancifulness, half humour and half pathos, that
soothed her tired senses like a lullaby.   Hence it
came to pass that the sole creature whom she loved
and who had pity for her was the uncouth, crippled,
gay, sad, gentle, dauntless creature whom his tribe
had always held half-wittol and half-seer.

Thus the life in the hills of the Liébana went on
till the child of Taric had entered her sixth year.

She had both beauty and grace ; she had the old
Moresco loveliness in its higher type ; she was fleet
as the roe, strong as the young izard, wild as the
wood-partridge on the wing ; she had grace of limb
from the postures and dances with which she taught
herself to keep time to the sweet, fantastic music of
the viol ; she was shy and sullen, and fierce and
savage, to all save himself, for the hand of every
other was against her ; but to him, she was docile as
the dove to the hand that feeds it.   He had given her

a string of bright sequins to hang on her hair, and when the peasants of the mountains and valleys saw her by the edge of some green woodland pool, whirling by moonlight to the sound of his melodies, they took her to be some unearthly spirit, and told wonderful things over their garlic of the elf crowned with stars they had seen dancing on a round lotus leaf in the hush of the night.

In the Liébana she was beaten often, hungry almost always, cursed fiercely, driven away by the mothers, mocked and flouted by the children ; and this taught her silence and ferocity. Yet in the Liébana she was happy, for one creature loved her, and she was free—free to lie in the long grass, to bathe in the still pools, to watch the wild things of the woods, to wander ankle deep in forest blossoms, to sleep under the rocking of pines, to run against the sweet force of the wind, to climb the trees and swing cradled in leaves, and to look far away at the snow on the mountains, and to dream, and to love, and to be content in dreaming and loving, their mystical glory that awoke with the sun.

One day in the red autumn, Taric came ; he had been wholly absent more than two years.

He was superb to the sight still, with matchless splendour of face and form, but his carriage was more reckless and disordered than ever, and in his gem-like and night-black eyes, there was a look of cunning and of subtle ferocity new to them.

His life had gone hardly with him, and to the indolence, the passions, the rapacity, the slothful sensuality of the gypsy—who had retained all the vices of his race whilst losing their virtues of simplicity in living, and of endurance under hardship—the gall of a sharp poverty had become unendurable : and to live without dice, and women, and wine, and boastful brawling, seemed to him to be worse than any death.

The day he returned, they were still camped in the Liébana ; in one of its narrow gorges, overhung with a thick growth of trees, and coursed through by a headlong hill-stream, that spread itself into darkling breadths and leafy pools, in which the fish were astir under great snowy lilies and a tangled web of water plants.

He strode into the midst of them, as they sat round their camp-fire lit beneath a shelf of rock, as his wont was ; and was welcomed and fed and plied with such as they had, with that mixture of sullen respect and incurable attachment which his tribe preserved, through all their quarrels, for this, the finest and the fiercest, the most fickle and the most faithless of them all.

He gorged himself, and drank, and said little.

When the meal was done, the young of the tribe scattered themselves in the red evening light under the great walnuts ; some at feud, some at play.

" Which is mine ? " he asked, surveying the children. They showed her to him. The sequins were round her head ; she swung on a bough of ash ; the pool beneath mirrored her ; she was singing as children sing, without words, yet musically and gladly, catching at the fireflies that danced above her in the leaves.

" Can she dance ? " he asked lazily of them.

" In her own fashion,—as a flower in the wind," Phratos answered him, with a smile ; and willing to woo for her the good graces of her father, he slung his viol off his shoulders and tuned it, and beckoned the child.

She came, knowing nothing who Taric was ; he was only to her a fierce-eyed man like the rest, who would beat her, most likely, if she stood between him and the sun, or overturned by mischance his horn of liquor.

Phratos played, and all the gypsy children, as their wont was, danced.

But she danced all alone, and with a grace and a fire that surpassed theirs. She was only a baby still; she had only her quick ear to guide her, and her only teacher was such inborn instinct as makes the birds sing and the young kids gambol.

Yet she danced with a wondrous subtlety and intensity of ardour beyond her years; her small brown limbs glancing like bronze in the fire-glow, the sequins flashing in her flying hair, and her form flung high in air, like a bird on the wing, or a leaf on the wind; never still, never ceasing to dart, and to leap, and to whirl, and to sway, yet always with a sweet dreamy indolence, even in her fiery unrest.

Taric watched her under his bent brow until the music ceased, and she dropped on the grass spent and panting like a swallow after a long ocean flight.

" She will do," he muttered.

" What is it you mean with the child ? " some women asked.

Taric laughed.

" The little vermin is good for a gold piece or two," he answered.

Phratos said nothing, but he heard.

After awhile the camp was still; the gypsies slept. Two or three of their men went out to try and harry cattle by the light of the moon if they should be in luck; two others went forth to set snares for the wood partridges and rabbits; the rest slumbered soundly, the dogs curled to a watching sleep of vigilant guard in their midst.

Taric alone sat by the dying fire. When all was very quiet, and the stars were clear in midnight skies, the woman Zarâ stole out of her tent to him.

"You signed to me," she said to him in a low voice. "You want the child killed?"

Taric showed his white teeth like a wolf.

"Not I; what should I gain?"

"What is it you want, then, with her?"

"I mean to take her, that is all. See here—a month ago, on the other side of the mountains, I met a fantoccini player. It was at a wine-shop, hard by Luzarches. He had a woman-child with him who danced to his music, and whom the people praised for her beauty, and who anticked like a dancing dog, and who made a great deal of silver. We got friends, he and I. At the week's end the brat died: some sickness of the throat, they said. Her master tore his hair and raved; the little wretch was worth handfuls of coin to him. For

such another he would give twelve gold pieces.   He
shall have her.   She will dance for him and me;
there is plenty to be made in that way.   The women
are fools over a handsome child; they open their
larders and their purses.   I shall take her away
before sunrise; he says he teaches them in seven
days, by starving and giving the stick.   She will
dance while she is a child.   Later on—there are the
theatres; she will be strong and handsome, and in
the great cities, now, a woman's comeliness is as a
mine of gold ore.   I shall take her away by sunrise."

"To sell her?"

The hard fierce heart of Zarâ rebelled against
him; she had no tenderness save for her own
offspring, and she had maltreated the stray child
many a time; yet the proud liberty and the savage
chastity of her race were roused against him by his
words.

Taric laughed again.

"Surely; why not?   I will make a dancing dog
of her for the peasants' pastime; and in time she
will make dancing dogs of the nobles and the
princes for her own sport.   It is a brave life—none
better."

The gypsy woman stood, astonished and irresolute.   If he had flung his child in the river, or

thrown her off a rock, he would have less offended
the instincts and prejudices of her clan.

"What will Phratos say?" she asked at length.

"Phratos? A rotten fig for Phratos! What can
he say—or do? The little beast is mine; I can
wring its neck if I choose, and if it refuse to pipe
when we play for it, I will."

The woman sought in vain to dissuade him; he
was inflexible. She left him at last, telling herself
that it was no business of hers. He had a right to
do what he chose with his own. So went and lay
down amongst her brown-faced boys, and was indifferent, and slept.

Taric likewise slept, upon a pile of moss under
the ledge of the rock, lulled by the heat of the fire,
which, ere lying down, he had fed with fresh boughs
of resinous wood.

When all was quite still, and his deep quiet
breathing told that his slumber was one not easily
broken, a man softly rose from the ground and threw
off a mass of dead leaves that had covered him, and
stood erect, a dark, strange, misshapen figure, in the
moonlight: it was Phratos.

He had heard, and understood all that Taric
meant for the present and the future of the child:
and he knew that when Taric vowed to do a thing

for his own gain, it were easier to uproot the chain of the Europa than to turn him aside from his purpose.

"It was my doing!" said Phratos to himself bitterly, as he stood there, and his heart was sick and sore in him, as with self-reproach for a crime.

He thought awhile, standing still in the hush of the midnight; then he went softly, with a footfall that did not waken a dog, and lifted up the skins of Zarâ's tent as they hung over the fir-poles. The moonbeams slanting through the foliage strayed in, and showed him the woman, sleeping among her rosy robust children, like a mastiff with her litter of tawny pups; and away from them, on the bare ground closer to the entrance, the slumbering form of the young daughter of Taric.

She woke as he touched her, opening bright bewildered eyes.

"Hush! it is I, Phratos," he murmured over her, and the stifled cry died on her lips.

He lifted her up in his arms and left the tent with her, and dropped the curtain of sheepskin, and went out into the clear, crisp, autumn night. Her eyes had closed again, and her head had sunk on his shoulder heavy with sleep; she had not tried to keep awake one moment after knowing that it was Phratos who had come for her; she loved him, and in his hold feared nothing.

Taric lay on the ledge of the rock, deaf with the torpor of a half-drunken slumber, dreaming gloomily; his hand playing in his dreams with the knife that was thrust in his waist-band.

Phratos stepped gently past him, and through the outstretched forms of the dogs and men, and across the died-out embers of the fire, over which the emptied soup-kettle still swung, as the night-breeze blew to and fro its chain. No one heard him.

He went out from their circle and down the path of the gorge in silence, carrying the child. She was folded in a piece of sheepskin, and in her hair there were still the sequins. They glittered in the white light as he went; as the wind blew, it touched the chords of the viol on his shoulder, and struck a faint musical sighing sound from them.

"Is it morning?" the child murmured, half asleep.

"No, dear; it is night," he answered her, and she was content and slept again—the strings of the viol sending a soft whisper in her drowsy ear, each time that the breeze arose and swept across them.

When the morning came it found him far on his road, leaving behind him the Liébana.

There followed a bright month of autumn weather. The child was happy as she had never been.

They moved on continually through the plains and the fields, the hills and the woods, the hamlets and the cities; but she and the viol were never weary. They rode aloft whilst he toiled on. Yet neither was he weary, for the viol murmured in the wind, and the child laughed in the sunshine.

It was late in the year.

The earth and sky were a blaze of russet and purple, and scarlet and gold. The air was keen and swift, and strong like wine. A summer fragrance blended with a winter frost. The grape harvest had been gathered in, and had been plentiful, and the people were liberal and of good humour.

Sometimes before a wine-shop or beneath a balcony, or in a broad market-square at evening, Phratos played; and the silver and copper coins were dropped fast to him. When he had enough by him to get a crust for himself, and milk and fruit for her, he did not pause to play, but moved on resolutely all the day, resting at night only.

He bought her a little garment of red foxes' furs; her head and her feet were bare. She bathed in clear running waters, and slept in a nest of hay. She saw vast towers, and wondrous spires, and strange piles of wood and stone, and rivers spanned by arches, and great forests half leafless, and plains red in stormy sunset light, and towns that lay hid in soft gold mists of vapour; and saw all these as in a dream, herself borne high in air, wrapped warm in fur, and lulled by the sweet familiar fraternity of the old viol. She asked no questions, she was content, like a mole or a dormouse; she was not beaten or mocked, she was never hungry nor cold; no one cursed her, and she was with Phratos.

It takes time to go on foot across a great country, and Phratos was nearly always on foot.

Now and then he gave a coin or two, or a tune or two, for a lift on some straw-laden waggon, or some mule-cart full of pottery or of vegetables, that was crawling on its slow way through the plains of the marshy lands, or the poplar-lined leagues of the public highways. But as a rule he plodded on by himself, shunning the people of his own race, and shunned in return by the ordinary populace of the places through which he travelled. For they knew him to be a Spanish gypsy by his skin and his garb and his language, and by the starry-eyed Arab-faced child who ran by his side in her red fur and her flashing sequins.

" There is a curse written against all honest folk on every one of those shaking coins," the peasants muttered as she passed them.

She did not comprehend their sayings, for she knew none but her gypsy tongue, and that only very imperfectly; but she knew by their glance that they meant that she was something evil; and she gripped tighter Phratos' hand —half-terrified, half-triumphant.

The weather grew colder and the ground harder. The golden and scarlet glories of the south and of the west, their red leafage and purple flowers, gorgeous sunsets and leaping waters, gave place to the level pastures, pale skies, leafless woods, and dim grey tints of the northerly lands.

The frosts became sharp, and mists that came from unseen seas enveloped them. There were marvellous old towns; cathedral spires that arose, ethereal as vapour; still dusky cities, aged with many centuries, that seemed to sleep eternally in the watery halo of the fog; green cultivated hills, from whose smooth brows the earth-touching clouds seemed never to lift themselves; straight sluggish streams, that flowed with leisurely laziness through broad flat meadow lands, white with snow and obscure with vapour. For these they had exchanged the pomp of dying foliage, the glory of crimson fruits, the fierce rush of the mistral, the odours of the noël-born violets, the fantastic shapes of the aloes and olives raising their dark spears and their silvery network against the amber fires of a winter dawn in the rich south-west.

The child was chilled, oppressed, vaguely awestruck, and disquieted; but she said nothing; Phratos was there and the viol.

She missed the red forests and the leaping torrents, and the prickly fruits, and the smell of the violets and the vineyards, and the wild shapes of the cactus, and the old myrtles that were hoary and contorted with age. But she did not complain nor ask any questions; she had supreme faith in Phratos.

One night, at the close of a black day in midwinter, the sharpest and hardest in cold that they had ever encountered, they passed through a little town whose roadways were mostly canals, and whose spires and roofs and pinnacles and turrets and towers were all beautiful with the poetry and the majesty of a long perished age.

The day had been bitter; there was snow everywhere; great blocks of ice choked up the water; the belfry chimes rang shrilly through the rarified air; the few folks that were astir were wrapped in wool or sheepskin; through the casements there glowed the ruddy flush of burning logs; and the muffled watchmen passing to and fro in antique custom on their rounds called out, under the closed houses, that it was eight of the night in a heavy snowstorm.

Phratos paused in the town at an old hostelry to give the child a hot drink of milk and a roll of rye bread. There he asked the way to the wood and the mill of Yprès.

They told it him sullenly and suspiciously: since for a wild gypsy of Spain the shrewd, thrifty, plain people of the north had no liking.

He thanked them, and went on his way, out of the barriers of the little town along a road by the river towards the country.

"Art thou cold, dear?" he asked her, with more tenderness than common in his voice.

The child shivered under her little fur skin, which would not keep out the searching of the hurricane and the driving of the snowflakes; but she drew her breath quickly, and answered him, "No."

They came to a little wood, leafless and black in the gloomy night; a dead crow swung in their faces on a swaying pear-tree; the roar of the mill-stream loudly filled what otherwise would have been an intense silence.

He made his way in by a little wicket, through an orchard and through a garden, and so to the front of the mill-house. The shutters were not closed; through the driving of the snow he could see within. It looked to him—a houseless wanderer from his youth up—strangely warm and safe and still.

An old man sat on one side of the wide hearth; an old woman, who span, on the other; the spinning-wheel turned, the thread flew, the logs smoked and flamed, the red glow played on the blue and white tiles of the chimney-place, and danced on the pewter and brass on the shelves; from the rafters there hung smoked meats and dried herbs and strings of onions; there was a crucifix, and below it a little Nativity, in wax and carved wood.

He could not tell that the goodly stores were only gathered there to be sold later at famine prices to a starving peasantry; he could not tell that the wooden god was only worshipped in a blind, bigoted, brutal selfishness, that desired to save its own soul, and to leave all other souls in eternal damnation.

He could not tell; he only saw old age and warmth, and comfort; and what the people who hooted him as a heathen called 'the religion of Love.

" They will surely be good to her ? " he thought. " Old people, and prosperous, and alone by their fireside."

It seemed that they must be so.

Any way, there was no other means to save her from Taric.

His heart was sore within him, for he had grown to love the child; and to the vagrant instincts of his race the life of the house and of the hearth seemed like the life of the cage for the bird. Yet Phratos, who was not altogether as his own people were, but had thought much and often in his own wild way, knew that such a life was the best for a woman child,—and, above all, for a woman child who had such a sire as Taric.

To keep her with himself was impossible. He had always dwelt with his tribe, having no life apart

from theirs; and even if he had left them, where-
ever he had wandered, there would Taric have followed, and found him, and claimed the child by his
right of blood. There was no other way to secure
her from present misery and future shame, save
only this; to place her with her mother's people.

She stood beside him, still and silent, gazing
through the snowflakes at the warmth of the mill-
kitchen within.

He stooped over her, and pushed between her
fur garment and her skin the letter he had found on
the breast of the dead woman in the Liébana.

"Thou wilt go in there to the old man yonder,
and sleep by that pleasant fire to-night," he murmured to her. "And thou wilt be good and gentle,
and even as thou art to me always; and to-morrow
at noontide I will come and see how it fares with
thee."

Her small hands tightened upon his.

"I will not go without thee," she muttered in
the broken tongue of the gipsy children.

There were food and milk, fire and shelter,
safety from the night and the storm there, she
saw; but these were nought to her without
Phratos. She struggled against her fate as the
young bird struggles against being thrust into the

cage,—not knowing what captivity means, and yet afraid of it and rebelling by instinct.

He took her up in his arms, and pressed her close to him, and for the first time kissed her. For Phratos, though tender to her, had no woman's foolishness, but had taught her to be hardy and strong, and to look for neither caresses nor compassion—knowing well that to the love child of Taric in her future years the first could only mean shame, and the last could only mean alms, which would be shame likewise.

"Go, dear," he said softly to her; and then he struck with his staff on the wooden door, and lifting its latch, unclosed it; and thrust the child forward, ere she could resist, into the darkness of the low entrance place.

Then he turned and went swiftly himself through the orchard and wood into the gloom and the storm of the night.

He knew that to show himself to a northern householder were to do her evil and hurt; for between the wanderer of the Spanish forests and the peasant of the Norman pastures there could be only defiance, mistrust, and disdain.

"I will see how it is with her to-morrow," he said to himself as he faced again the wind

and the sleet. "If it, be well with her—let it
be well. If not, she must come forth with me,
and we must seek some lair where her wolf-sire
shall. not prowl and discover her. But it will
be hard to find; for the vengeance of Taric is
swift of foot and has a far-stretching hand and
eyes that are sleepless."

And his heart was heavy in him as he went.
He had done what seemed to him just and due to
the child and her mother; he had been true to the
vow he had made answering the mute prayer of the
sightless dead eyes; he had saved the flesh of the
child from the whip of the trainer, and the future
of the child from the shame of the brothel; he
had done thus much in saving her from her father,
and he had done it in the only way that was
possible to him.

Yet his heart was heavy as he went; and it
seemed to him even as though he had thrust
some mountain bird with pinions that would
cleave the clouds, and eyes that would seek the
sun, and a song that would rise with the dawn, and
a courage that would breast the thunder, down into
the darkness of a trap, to be shorn and crippled
and silenced for evermore.

"I will see her to-morrow," he told himself

restless with a vague remorse, as though the good he had done had been evil.

But when the morrow dawned there had happened that to Phratos which forbade him to see whether it were well with her that day or any day in all the many years that came.

For Phratos that night, being blinded and shrouded in the storm of snow, lost such slender knowledge as he had of that northern country, and wandered far afield, not knowing where he was in the wide white desert, on which no single star-ray shone.

The violence of the storm grew with the hours. The land was a sheet of snow. The plains were dim and trackless as a desert. Sheep were frozen in their folds, and cattle drowned amidst the ice in the darkness. All lights were out, and the warning peals of the bells were drowned in the tempest of the winds.

The land was strange to him, and he lost all knowledge where he was. Above, beneath, around, were the dense rolling clouds of snow. Now and then through the tumult of the hurricane there was blown a strange harsh burst of jangled chimes that wailed a moment loudly on the silence and then died again.

At many doors he knocked : the doors of little lonely places standing in the great colourless waste.

But each door, being opened cautiously, was with haste shut in his face again.

"It is a gypsy," the people muttered, and were afraid ; and they drew their bars closer and huddled together in their beds, and thanked their saints that they were safe beneath a roof.

He wrapped his sheepskin closer round him and set his face against the blast.

A hundred times he strove to set his steps backwards to the town, and a hundred times he failed ; and moved only round and round vainly, never escaping the maze of the endless white fields.

Now the night was long, and he was weakly.

In the midst of the fields there was a cross, and at the head of the cross hung a lantern. The wind tossed the light to and fro. It flickered on the head of a woman. She lay in the snow, and her hand grasped his foot as he passed her.

"I am dead," she said to him : " dead of hunger. But the lad lives—save him."

And as she spoke, her lips closed together and her throat rattled, and she died.

The boy slept at her feet, and babbled in his sleep, delirious.

Phratos stooped down and raised him. He was a child of eight years, and worn with famine and fever, and his gaunt eyes stared hideously up at the driving snow.

Phratos folded him in his arms, and went on with him : the snow had nearly covered the body of his mother.

All around were the fields. There was no light, except from the lantern on the cross. A few sheep huddled near without a shepherd. The stillness was intense. The bells had ceased to ring or he had wandered far from the sound of them.

The lad was senseless ; he muttered drearily foolish words of fever ; his limbs hung in a dead weight ; his teeth chattered. Phratos, bearing him, struggled on : the snow was deep and drifted heavily ; every now and then he stumbled and plunged to his knees in a rift of earth or in a shallow pool of ice.

At last his strength, feeble at all times, failed him ; his arms could bear their burden no longer ; he let the young boy slip from his hold upon the ground ; and stood, breathless and broken, with the snowflakes beating on him.

" The woman trusted me," he thought ; she was a stranger, she was a beggar, she was dead. She had no bond upon him, neither could she ever bear witness against him. Yet he was loyal to her.

He unwound the sheepskin that he wore, and stripped himself of it and folded it about the sick child, and with a slow laborious effort drew the little body away under the frail shelter of a knot of furze, and wrapped it closely round, and left it there.

It was all that he could do.

Then, with no defence between him and the driving cold, he strove once more to find his road.

It was quite dark ; quite still.

The snow fell ceaselessly ; the white wide land was pathless as the sea.

He stumbled on as a mule may that being blind and bruised yet holds its way from the sheer instinct of its sad dumb patience.

His veins were frozen ; his beard was ice ; the wind cut his flesh like a scourge ; a sickly dreamy sleepiness stole on him.

He knew well what it meant.

He tried to rouse himself; he was young, and

his life had its sweetness; and there were faces he would fain have seen again, and voices whose laughter he would fain have heard.

He drew the viol round and touched its strings; but his frozen fingers had lost their cunning, and the soul of the music was chilled and dumb: it only sighed in answer.

He kissed it softly as he would have kissed a woman's lips, and put it in his bosom. It had all his youth in it.

Then he stumbled onward yet again, feebly, being a cripple and cold to the bone, and pierced with a million thorns of pain.

There was no light anywhere.

The endless wilderness of the ploughed lands stretched all around him; where the little hamlets clustered the storm hid them; no light could penetrate the denseness of that changeless gloom; and the only sound that rose upon the ghastly silence was the moaning of some perishing flock locked in a flood of ice, and deserted by its shepherd.

But what he saw and what he heard were not these; going barefoot and blindfold to his death, the things of his own land were with him; the golden glories of sunsets of paradise; the scarlet blaze of a wilderness of flowers ; the sound of the fountains at midnight ; the glancing of the swift feet in the dances ; the sweetness of songs sad as death sung in the desolate courts of old palaces ; the deep dreamy hush of white moons shining through lines of palms straight on a silvery sea. These arose and drifted before him, and he ceased to suffer or to know, and sleep conquered him ; and he dropped down on the earth noise-lessly and powerlessly as a leaf sinks ; and the snow fell and covered him.

When the morning broke a peasant, going to his labour in the fields while the stormy winter sun rose red over the whitened world, found both his body and the child's.

The boy was warm and living still beneath the shelter of the sheepskin : Phratos was dead.

The people succoured the child, and nursed and fed him so that his life was saved ; but to Phratos they only gave such burial as the corby gives the stricken deer.

"It is only a gypsy ; let him lie," they said ; and they left him there, and the snow kept him.

His viol they robbed him of, and cast it as a plaything to their children. But the children could make no melody from its dumb strings.

For the viol was faithful; and its music was dead too.

And his own land and his own people knew him never again; and never again at evening was the voice of his viol heard in the stillness; and never again did the young men and maidens dance to his bidding, and the tears and the laughter rise and fall at his will, and the beasts and the birds frisk and sing at his coming, and the children in his footsteps cry :—" Lo, it is summer, since Phratos is here!"

BOOK II.

"Yo contra todos, y todos contra yo."

CHAPTER I.

THE hottest sun of a hot summer shone on a straight dusty road. An old man was breaking stones by the wayside; he was very old, very bent, very lean, worn by ninety years if he had been worn by one; but he struck yet with a will, and the flints flew in a thousand pieces under his hammer, as though the youth and the force of nineteen years instead of ninety were at work on them.

When the noon bell rang from a little odd straight steeple, with a slanting roof, that peered out of the trees to the westward, he laid his hammer aside, threw off his brass-plated cap, wiped his forehead of its heat and dust, sat down on his pile of stones, and took out a hard black crust and munched it with teeth that were still strong and white.

The noontide was very quiet; the heat was intense, for there had been no rainfall for several weeks; there was one lark singing high up in the air, with its little breast lifted to the sun; but all the other birds were mute and invisible, doubtless hidden safely in some delicious shadow, swinging drowsily on tufts of linden bloom, or underneath the roofing of broad chestnut leaves.

The road on either side was lined by the straight forms of endless poplars, standing side by side as sentinels. The fields were all ablaze on every acre with the gold of ripening corn or mustard, and the scarlet flame of innumerable poppies. Here and there they were broken by some little house, white or black, or painted in bright colours, which lifted up amongst its leaves a little tower like a sugar-loaf, or a carved gable, and a pointed arch beneath it. Now and then they were divided by rows of trees standing breathless in the heat, or breadths of apple orchards, some with early fruits already ripe, some with fruits as yet green as their foliage.

Through it all the river ran, silver in the light; with shallow fords, where the deep-flanked bullocks drank; and ever and anon an ancient picturesque bridge of wood, time-bronzed and moss-embedded.

The old man did not look round once ; he had been on these roads a score of years ; the place had to him the monotony and colourlessness 'which all long familiar scenes wear to the eyes that are weary of them.

He was ninety-five; he had to labour for his living ; he ate black bread ; he had no living kith or kin ; no friend save in the mighty legion of the dead ; and he sat in the scorch of the sun ; he hated the earth and the sky, the air and the landscape : why not ? They had no loveliness for him ; he only knew that the flies stung him, and that the red ants could crawl through the holes in his shoes, and bite him sharply with their little piercing teeth.

He sat in such shade as the tall lean poplar gave, munching his hard crusts ; he had a fine keen profile and a long white beard that were thrown out as sharply as sculpture against the golden sunlight, in which the gnats were dancing. His eyes were fastened on the dust as he ate ; blue piercing eyes that had still something of the fire of their youth ; and his lips under the white hair moved a little now and then, half audibly.

His thoughts were with the long dead years of an unforgotten time—a time that will be remembered as long as the earth shall circle round the sun.

With the present he had nothing to do; he worked to satisfy the lingering cravings of a body that age seemed to have lost all power to kill; he worked because he was too much of a man still to beg, and because suicide looked to his fancy like a weakness, but life for all that was over with him; life in the years of his boyhood had been a thing so splendid, so terrible, so drunken, so divine, so tragic, so intense, that the world seemed now to him to have grown pale and grey and pulseless, with no sap in its veins, no hue in its suns, no blood in its humanity.

For his memory held the days of Thermidor; the weeks of the White Terror; the winter dawn, when the drums rolled out a King's threnody; the summer nights, when all the throats of Paris cried "Marengo!"

He had lived in the wondrous awe of that abunddant time when every hour was an agony or a victory; when every woman was a martyr or a bacchanal; when the same scythe that had severed the flowering grasses served also to cleave the fair breasts of the mother, the tender throat of the child; when the ground was purple with the blue blood of men as with the juices of out-trodden grapes, and when the waters were white with the bodies of virgins as

with the moon-fed lilies of summer. And now he
sat here by the wayside, in the dust and the sun,
only feeling the sting of the fly and the bite of the
ant ; and the world seemed dead to him, because so
long ago, though his body still lived on, his soul had
cursed God and died.

Through the golden motes of the dancing air and
of the quivering sunbeams, whilst high above the lark
sang on, there came along the road a girl.

She was bare-footed and bare-throated, lithe of
movement, and straight and supple, as one who
passed her life on the open lands and was abroad
in all changes of the weather.

She walked with the free and fearless measure of
the country women of Rome or the desert-born
women of Nubia ; she had barely entered her
sixteenth year, but her bosom and limbs were full
and firm, and moulded with almost all the luxuriant
splendour of maturity ; her head was not covered
after the fashion of the country, but had a scarlet
kerchief wound about, and on it she bore a great
flat basket, filled high with fruits and herbs and
flowers ; a mass of colour and of blossom, through
whose leaves and tendrils her dark level brows and
her great eyes, blue black as a tempestuous night,
looked out, set straight against the sun.

She came on, treading down the dust with her long and slender feet, that were such feet as a sculptor would give to his Cleopatra or his Phryne. Her face was grave, shadowed, even fierce ; and her mouth, though scarlet as a berry and full and curled, had its lips pressed close on one another, like the lips of one who has long kept silence, and may keep it—until death.

As she saw the old man her eyes changed and lightened with a smile which for the moment banished all the gloom and savage patience from her eyes, and made them mellow and lustrous as a southern sun.

She paused before him, and spoke, showing her beautiful white teeth, small and even, like rows of cowrie shells.

"You are well, Marcellin ?"

The old man started, and looked up with a certain gladness on his own keen visage, which had lost all expression save such as an intense and absorbed retrospection will lend.

"Fool!" he made answer, harshly yet not unkindly. "When will you know that so long as an old man lives so long it cannot be 'well' with him ?"

"Need one be a man, or old, to answer so ?"

She spoke in the accent and the language of the province, but with a voice rich and pure and cold; not the voice of the north, or of any peasantry. She put her basket down from off her head, and leaned against the trunk of the poplar beside him, crossing her arms upon her bare chest.

"To the young everything is possible; to the old nothing," he said curtly.

Her eyes gleamed with a fierce thirsty longing; she made him no reply.

He broke off half his dry bread and tendered it to her. She shook her head and motioned it away; yet she was as hungered as any hawk that has hunted all through the night and the woods, and has killed nothing. The growing life, the superb strength, the lofty stature of her made her need constant nourishment, as young trees need it; and she was fed as scantily as a blind beggar's dog, and less willingly than a galley slave.

The kindly air had fed her richly, strongly, continually; that was all.

"Possible!" she said slowly, after awhile. "What is possible? I do not understand."

The old man, Marcellin, smiled grimly.

"You see that lark? It soars there, and sings there. It is possible that a fowler may hide in the

grasses; it is possible that it may be shot as it
sings; it is possible that it may have the honour to
die in agony to grace a rich man's table.   You
see?"

She mused a moment; her brain was rapid in
intuitive perception, but barren of all culture; it
took her many moments to follow the filmy track of
a metaphorical utterance.   But by degrees she saw
his meaning, and the shadow settled over her face
again.

"The possible, then, is only—the worse?" she
said slowly.

The old man smiled still grimly.

"Nay; our friends the priests say there is a
'possible' which will give—one day—the fowler who
kills the lark the wings of the lark, and the lark's
power to sing *Laus Deo* in heaven.   *I* do not say—
they do."

"The priests!"

All the scorn of which her curved lips were
capable curled on them, and a deep hate gathered
in her eyes—a hate that was unfathomable and
mute.

"Then there is no 'possible' for me," she said
bitterly, "if so be that priests hold the gifts
of it?"

Marcellin looked up at her from under his bushy white eyebrows; a glance fleet and keen as the gleam of blue steel.

"Yes, there is," he said curtly. "You are a woman child, and have beauty : the devil will give you one."

"Always the devil!" she muttered. There was impatience in her echo of the words, and yet there was an awe also as of one who uses a name that is mighty and full of majesty, although familiar.

"Always the devil!" repeated Marcellin. "For the world is always of men."

His meaning this time lay too deep for her, and passed her; she stood leaning against the poplar, with her head bent and her form motionless in the sunlight like a statue of bronze.

"If men be devils they are my brethren," she said suddenly; "why do they then so hate me?"

The old man stroked his beard.

"Because Fraternity is Hate. Cain said so; but God would not believe him."

She mused over the saying; silent still.

The lark dropped down from heaven, suddenly falling through the air, mute. It had been struck by a sparrow-hawk, which flashed black against the azure of the skies and the white haze of the atmo-

sphere ; and which flew down in the track of the
lark and seized it ere it gained the shelter of the
grass and bore it away within his talons.

Marcellin pointed to it with his pipe-stem.

"You see there are many forms of the 'possible' "——

"When it means Death," she added.

The old man took his pipe back and smoked.

"Of course, Death is the key-note of creation."

Again she did not comprehend ; a puzzled pain
clouded the lustre of her eyes.

"But the lark praised God—why should it be
so dealt with ?"

Marcellin smiled grimly.

"Abel was praising God ; but that did not turn
aside the steel."

She was silent yet again ; he had told her that
old story of the sons born of Eve, and the one
whom, hearing it, she had understood and pitied
had been Cain.

At that moment, through the roadway that wound
across the meadows and through the corn lands and
the trees, there came in sight a gleam of scarlet
that was not from the poppies, a flash of silver that
was not from the river, a column of smoke that was
not from the weeds that burned on the hillside.

There came a cloud, with a melodious murmur softly rising from it; a cloud that moved
between the high flowering hedges, the tall amber
wheat, the slender poplars, and the fruitful orchards;
a cloud that grew larger and clearer as it drew more
near to them, and left the green water meadows
and the winding field paths for the great high
road.

It was a procession of the Church.

It drew closer and closer by slow imperceptible
degrees, until it approached them; the old man sat
upright, not taking his cap from his head nor his
pipe from his mouth; the young girl ceased to lean
for rest against the tree, and stood with her arms
crossed on her breast.

The Church passed them; the great gilt crucifix
held aloft, the scarlet and the white of the floating
robes catching the sunlight; the silver chains and
silver censers gleaming; the fresh young voices
of the singing children cleaving the air like a rush
of wind; the dark shorn faces of the priests
bowed over open books, the tender sound of little
bells ringing across the low deep monotony of
prayer.

The Church passed them; the dust of the parched
road rose up in a choking mass; the heavy mist

of the incense hung darkly on the sunlit air; the
tramp of the many feet startled the birds from
their rest, and pierced through the noonday
silence.

It passed them, and left them behind it; but the
fresh leaves were choked and whitened; the birds
were fluttered and affrightened; the old man
coughed, the girl strove to brush the dust motes
from her smarting eyelids.

"That is the Church!" said the stone-breaker,
with a smile. "Dust—terror—a choked voice—
and blinded eyes."

Now she understood; and her beautiful curled
lips laughed mutely.

The old man rammed some more tobacco into the
bowl of his pipe.

"That is the Church!" he said. "To burn incense and pray for rain, and to fell the forests that
were the rain-makers."

The procession passed away out of sight, going
along the highway and winding by the course of
the river, calling to the bright blue heavens for
rain; whilst the little bells rang and the incense
curled and the priests prayed themselves hoarse,
and the peasants toiled footsore, and the eager
steps of the choral children trod the tiny gnat

dead in the grasses and the bright butterfly dead in the dust.

The priests had cast a severer look from out their down-dropped eyelids; the children had huddled together, with their voices faltering a little; and the boy choristers had shot out their lips in gestures of defiance and opprobrium as they had passed these twain beneath the wayside trees. For the two were both outcasts.

" Didst thou see the man that killed the king?" whispered to another one fair and curly-headed baby, who was holding in the sun her little, white, silver-fringed banner, and catching the rise and fall of the sonorous chaunt as well as she could with her little, lisping tones.

" Didst thou see the daughter of the devil?" muttered to another a handsome golden brown boy, who had left his herd untended in the meadow to don his scarlet robes and swing about the censer of his village chapel.

And they all sang louder, and tossed more incense on high, and marched more closely together under the rays of the gleaming crucifix as they went; feeling that they had been beneath the shadow of the powers of darkness, and that they were purer and holier and more exalted, because

K 2

they had thus passed by in scorn what was accursed
with psalms on their lips, with the cross as their
symbol.

So they went their way through the peaceful
country with a glory of sunbeams about them—
through the corn, past the orchards, by the river,
into the heart of the old brown, quiet town, and
about the foot of the great cathedral, where they
kneeled down in the dust and prayed, then rose and
sang the " Angelus."

Then, the tall dark-visaged priest, who had led
them all thither under the standard of the golden
crucifix, lifted his voice alone and implored God,
and exhorted man ; implored for rain and all the
blessings of harvest, exhorted to patience and the
imitation of God.

The people were moved and saddened, and listened, smiting their breasts ; and after a while rising
from their knees, many of them in tears, dis-
persed and went their ways, muttering to one
another:—" We have had no such harvests as those
of old since the man that slew a saint came to
dwell here ; " and answering to one another:—
" We had never such droughts as these in the
sweet cool weather of old, before the offspring of
hell was amongst us."

For the priests had not said to them, "Lo! your mercy is parched as the earth, and your hearts as the heavens are brazen."

CHAPTER II.

IN the days of his youngest youth, in the old drunken days that were dead, this old stone-breaker Marcellin had known such life as it is given to few men to know—a life of the soul and the senses; a life of storm and delight; a life mad with blood and with wine; a life of divinest dreams; a life when women kissed them, and bade them slay; a life when mothers blessed them and bade them die; a life, strong, awful, splendid, unutterable; a life seized at its fullest and fiercest and fairest, out of an air that was death, off an earth that was hell.

When his cheeks had had a boy's bloom and his curls a boy's gold he had seen a nation in delirium; he had been one of the elect of a people; he had uttered the words that burn, and wrought the acts that live; he had been of the Thousand of

Marsala; and he had been of the avengers in
Thermidor: he had raised his flute-like voice from
the tribune, and he had cast in his vote for the
death of a king; passions had been his playthings,
and he had toyed with life as a child with a match;
he had beheld the despised enthroned in power,
and desolation left within kings' palaces; he too
had been fierce, and glad, and cruel, and gay, and
drunken, and proud, as the whole land was; he
had seen the white beauty of royal women bare
in the hands of the mob, and the throats that
princes had caressed kissed by the broad steel
knife; he had had his youth in a wondrous time,
when all men had been gods or devils, and all
women martyrs or furies.

And now,—he broke stones to get daily bread,
and those who passed him by cursed him, saying:
" This man slew a king."

For he had outlived his time, and the life that
had been golden and red at its dawn was now grey
and pale as the ashes of a fire grown cold; for in
all the list of the world's weary errors there is no
mistake so deadly as age.

Years before, in such hot summer weather as this
against which the Church had prayed, the old man,
going homewards to his little cabin amidst the

fields, had met a little child coming straight towards him in the full crimson glow of the setting sun, and with the flame of the poppies all around her.

He hardly knew why he looked at her, but when he had once looked his eyes rested there.

She had the hues of his youth about her; in that blood-red light, amongst the blood-red flowers, she made him think of women's forms that he had seen in all their grace and their voluptuous loveliness clothed in the red garment of death, and standing on the dusky red of the scaffold as the burning mornings of the summers of slaughter had risen over the land.

The child was all alone before him in that intense glow as of fire; above her there was a tawny sky, flushed here and there with purple; around here stretched the solitary level of the fields burnt yellow as gold by the long months of heat. There were stripes on her shoulders blue and black from the marks of a thong.

He looked at her, and stopped her, why he hardly knew, except that a look about her, beaten but yet unsubdued, attracted him. He had seen the look of yore in the years of his youth, on the faces of the nobles he hated.

"Have you been hurt?" he asked her in his

harsh, strong voice. She put her heavy load of faggots down and stared at him.

"Hurt?" She echoed the word stupidly. No one ever thought she could be hurt; what was done to her was punishment and justice.

"Yes. Those stripes—they must be painful?"

She gave a gesture of assent with her head, but she did not answer.

"Who beat you?" he pursued.

A cloud of passion swept over her bent face.

"Flamma."

"You were wicked?"

"They said so."

"And what do you do when you are beaten?"

"I shut my mouth."

"For what?"

"For fear they should know it hurt me—and be glad."

Marcellin leaned on his elm stick, and fastened on her his keen passionless eyes with a look which, for him who shunned and was shunned by all his kind, was almost sympathy.

"Come to my hut," he said to her. "I know a herb that will take the fret and the ache out of your bruises."

The child followed him passively, half stupidly;
he was the first creature that had ever bidden her
go with him, and this rough pity of his was sweet to
her, with an amazing incredible balm in it which
only those can know who see raised against them
every man's hand, and hear on their ears the
mockery of all the voices of their world.

Under reviling, and contempt, and constant rejec-
tion, she had become savage as a trapped hawk,
wild as an escaped panther; but to him she was
obedient and passive, because he had spoken to her
without a taunt and without a curse, which until
now had been the sole two forms of human speech
that she had heard.

His little hut was in the midst of those spreading cornfields, set where two pathways crossed
each other, and stretched down the gentle slope
of the cultured lands to join the great highway
—a hut of stones and plaited rushes, with a
roof of thatch, where the old republican, hardy
of frame and born of a toiling race, dwelt in soli-
tude, and broke his scanty bitter bread without
lament, if without content.

He took some leaves of a simple herb that he
knew, soaked them with water, and bound them on
her shoulders, not ungently, though his hand was

so rough with labour, and, as men said, had been so often red with carnage.

Then he gave her a draught of goat's milk, sweet and fresh, from a wooden bowl; shared with her the dry black crusts that formed his only evening meal; bestowed on her a gift of a rare old scarlet scarf of woven wools and eastern broideries, one of the few relics of his buried life; lifted the faggots on her back, so that she could carry them with greater ease; and set her on her homeward way.

"Come to me again," he said, briefly, as she went across the threshold.

The child bent her head in silence, and kissed his hand quickly and timidly, like a grateful dog that is amazed to have a caress, and not a blow.

"After a forty years' vow I have broken it; I have pitied a human thing," the old man muttered as he stood in his doorway looking after her shadow as it passed small and dark across the scarlet light of the poppies.

"They call him vile, and they say that he slew men," thought the child, who had long known his face, though he never had noted hers; and it seemed to her that all mercy lay in her father's kingdom—which they called the kingdom of evil.

The cool moist herbs slaked the heat of her bruises ; and the draught of milk had slaked the thirst of her throat.

" Is evil good ? " she asked in her heart as she went through the tall red poppies.

And from that evening thenceforward Folle-Farine and Marcellin cleaved to one another, being outcasts from all others.

CHAPTER III.

AS the religious gathering broke up and split in divers streams to divers ways, the little town returned to its accustomed stillness— a stillness that seemed to have in it the calm of a thousand sleeping years, and the legends and the dreams of half a score of old dead centuries.

On market-days and saint-days, days of high feast or of perpetual chaffering, the town was full of colour, movement, noise, and population.

The country people crowded in, filling it with the jingling of mule-bells; the fisher people came, bringing in with them the crisp salt smell of the sea and the blue of the sea on their garments; its own tanners and ivory carvers, and fruiterers, and lacemakers turned out by the hundred in all the quaint variety of costumes which their forefathers had bequeathed to them, and to which they were still wise enough to adhere. But at other times when the fishers were in their hamlets, and the peasantry on their lands and in their orchards, and the townsfolk at their labours in the old rich renaissance mansions which they had turned into tanneries, and granaries, and wool-sheds, and workshops, the place was profoundly still; scarcely a child at play in the streets, scarcely a dog asleep in the sun.

When the crowds had gone the priests laid aside their vestments, and donned the black serge of their daily habit, and went to their daily avocations in their humble dwellings.

The crosses and the censers were put back upon their altars, and hung up upon their pillars.

The boy choristers and the little children put their white linen and their scarlet robes back in cupboards and presses, with heads of lavender and sprigs of rosemary to keep the moth and the devil away, and went to their fields, to their homes, to their herds, to their paper kites, to their daisy chains, to the poor rabbits they pent in a hutch, to the poor flies they killed in the sun.

The town became quite still, the market-place quite empty; the drowsy silence of a burning, cloudless afternoon was over all the quiet places about the cathedral walls, where of old the bishops and the canons dwelt; grey shady courts; dim open cloisters; houses covered with oaken carvings, and shadowed with the spreading branches of chestnuts and of lime-trees that were as aged as themselves.

Under the shelter of one of the lindens, after the populace had gone, there was seated on a broad stone bench the girl who had stood by the wayside erect and unbending as the procession had moved before her.

She had flung herself down in dreamy restfulness. She had delivered her burden of vegetables and fruit at a shop near by, whose awning stretched out into the street like a toadstool yellow with the sun. The heat was intense; she had been on foot all day; she sat to rest a moment, and put her burning hands under a little rill of water that spouted into a basin in a niche in the wall. An ancient well, with a stone image of the Madonna sculptured above, and a wreath of vine-leaves in stone running around, in the lavish ornamentation of an age when men loved loveliness for its own sake, and begrudged neither time nor labour in its service.

She leaned over the fountain, kept so cool by

the roofing of the thick green leaves; there was a metal cup attached to the basin by a chain, and she filled it at the running thread of water, and stooped her lips to it again and again thirstily.

The day was sultry; the ways were long and white with powdered limestone; her throat was still parched with the dust raised by the many feet of the multitude; and although she had borne in the great basket which now stood empty at her side, cherries, peaches, mulberries, melons, full of juice and lusciousness, this daughter of the devil had not taken even one to freshen her dry mouth.

Folle-Farine stooped to the water and played with it, and drank it, and steeped her lips and her arms in it; lying there on the stone bench, with her bare feet curled one in another, and her slender round limbs full of the voluptuous repose of a resting panther. The coolness, the murmur, the clearness, the peace, the soft flowing movement of water, possess an ineffable charm for natures that are passion-tossed, feverish, and full of storm.

There was a dreamy peace about the place, too, which had charms likewise for her; in the dusky arch of the long cloisters, in the grey lichen-grown walls, in the broad pamments of the paven court, in the clusters of strange delicate carvings beneath and below ; in the sculptured friezes where little nests that the birds had made in the spring still rested, and in the dense brooding thickness of the boughs which brought the sweetness and the shadows of the woods into the heart of the peopled town.

She stayed there, loath to move ; loath to return where a jeer, a bruise, a lifted stick, a muttered curse, were all her greeting and her guerdon.

As she lay thus, one of the doors in the old houses in the cloisters opened; the head of an old woman was thrust out, crowned with the high fan-shaped comb, and the towering white linen cap, that are the female note of that especial town.

The old woman was the mother of the sacristan, and she, looking out, shrieked shrilly to her son :

" Georges, Georges ! come hither. The devil's daughter is drinking the blest water ! "

The sacristan was hoeing amongst his cabbages in the garden behind his house, surrounded with clipt yew, and damp from the deep shade of the cathedral, that overshadowed it.

He ran out at his mother's call, hoe in hand, himself an old man, though stout and strong.

The well in the wall was his especial charge and pride ; immeasurable sanctity attached to it.

According to tradition, the water had spouted from the stone itself, at the touch of a branch of blossoming pear, held in the hand of St. Jerome, who had returned to earth in the middle of the four-teenth century, and dwelt for a while near the cathedral, working at the honourable trade of a cordwainer, and accomplishing mighty miracles throughout the district. It was said that some of his miraculous power still remained in the fountain, and that even yet, those who drank on St. Jerome's day, in full faith and with believing hearts, were, oftentimes, cleansed of sin, and purified of bodily disease.

Wherefore on that day, throngs of peasantry flocked in from all sides, and crowded round it, and drank; to the benefit of the sacristan in charge, if not to that of their souls and bodies.

Summoned by his mother, he flew to the rescue of the sanctified spring.

" Get you gone ! " he shouted. " Get you gone, you child of hell ! How durst you touch the blessed basin ? Do you think that God struck water from the stone for such as you ? "

Folle-Farine lifted her head and looked him in the face with her audacious eyes, and laughed ; then tossed her head again, and plunged it into the bright living water, till her lips, and her cheeks, and all the rippling hair about her temples sparkled with its silvery drops.

The sacristan, infuriated at once by the impiety and the defiance, shrieked aloud.

"Insolent animal! Daughter of Satan! I will teach you to taint the gift of a saint with lips of the devil!"

And he seized her roughly with one hand upon her shoulder, and with the other raised the hoe and brandished the wooden staff of it above her head in threat to strike her; whilst his old mother, still thrusting her lofty headgear and her wrinkled face from out the door, screamed to him to show he was a man, and have no mercy.

As his grasp touched her, and the staff cast its shadow across her, Folle-Farine sprang up, defiance and fury breathing from all her beautiful fierce face.

She seized the staff in her right hand, wrenched it with a swift movement from his hold, and catching his head under her left arm, rained blows on him from his own weapon, with a sudden gust of breathless rage which blinded him, and lent to her slender muscular limbs, the strength and the force of man. Then, as rapidly as she had seized and struck him, she flung him from her with such violence that he fell prostrate on the pavement of the court; caught up the metal pail which stood by ready filled, dashed the water over him where he lay, and turning from him without a word, walked across the courtyard slowly, and with a haughty grace in all the carriage of her bare limbs, and the folds of her ragged garments; bearing the empty osier basket on her head, deaf as the stones around to the screams of the sacristan and his mother.

In these secluded cloisters, and in the high noontide, when all were sleeping or eating in the cool shelter of their darkened houses, the old woman's voice remained unheard.

The saints heard, no doubt, but they were too lazy to stir from their niches in that sultry noontide; except the baying of a chained dog aroused, there was no answer to the outcry, and Folle-Farine passed out into the market place unarrested, and not meeting another living creature.

As she turned into one of the squares that led to the open country, she saw in the distance one of the guardians of the peace of the town moving quickly towards the cloisters, with his glittering lace shining in the sun, and his long scabbard clattering upon the stones. She laughed a little as she saw.

" They will not come after *me*," she said to herself. " They are too afraid of the devil."

She judged rightly; they did not come.

She crossed all the wide scorching square, whose
white stones blazed in the glare of the sun.

There was nothing in sight except a stray cat
prowling in a corner, and three sparrows quarrelling
over a foul-smelling heap of refuse.

The quaint old houses round seemed all asleep,
with the shutters closed like tired eyelids over
their little, dim, aged, orbs of windows. The
gilded vanes on their twisted chimneys, and carved
parapets, pointed motionless to the warm south.
There was not a sound, except the cawing of some
rooks, who built their nests high aloft in the
fretted pinnacles of the cathedral.

Undisturbed she crossed the square, and took her
way down the crooked street that led her homeward to the outlying country. It was· an old,
twisting, dusky place, with the water flowing through
its centre as its only roadway ; and in it there were
the oldest houses of the town, all of timber, black
with age, and carved with the wonderful florid
fancies and grotesque conceits of the years when a
house was to its master a thing beloved and beautiful, a bulwark, an altar, a heritage, an heirloom to

be dwelt in all the days of a long life, and bequeathed in all honour and honesty to a noble offspring.

The street was very silent, the ripple of the water was the chief sound that filled it. Its tenants were very poor, and in many of its antique mansions the beggars shared shelter with the rats and the owls. In one of these dwellings, however, there were still some warmth and colour.

The orange and scarlet flowers of a nasturtium curled up its twisted pilasters; the big, fair clusters of hydrangea filled up its narrow casements; a breadth of many-coloured saxifrage, with leaves of green and rose, and blossoms of purple and white, hung over the balcony rail, which five centuries earlier had been draped with cloth of gold; and a little yellow song bird made music in the empty niche from which the sculptured flower-de-luce had been so long torn down.

From that window a woman looked, leaning with folded arms above the rose-tipped saxifrage, and beneath the green-leaved vine.

She was a fair woman, white as the lilies, and she had silver pins in her amber hair, and a mouth that laughed sweetly. She called to Folle-Farine,

"You brown thing; why do you stare at me?"

Folle-Farine started and withdrew the fixed gaze of her lustrous eyes.

"Because you are beautiful," she answered curtly.

All beautiful things had a fascination for her. This woman above was very fair to see, and she looked at her as she looked at the purple butterflies in the sun; at the stars shining down through the leaves; at the vast, dim, gorgeous figures in the cathedral windows; at the happy children running to their mothers with their hands full of primroses, as she saw them in the woods at spring-time; at the laughing groups round the wood-fires in the new year time when she passed a lattice pane that the snow-drift had not blocked; at all the things that were so often in her sight, and yet with which her life had no part or likeness.

She stood there on the rough flints, in the darkness cast from the jutting beams of the house; and the other happier creature leaned above there in the light, white and rose-hued, and with the silver bells of the pins shaking in her yellow tresses.

"You are old Flamma's grand-daughter," cried the other, from her leafy nest above. "You work for him all day long at the mill?"

"Yes."

"And your feet are bare, and your clothes are rags,

and you go to and fro like a packhorse, and the
people hate you? You must be a fool. Your father
was the devil, they say: why do you not make him
give you good things?"

"He will not hear," the child muttered wearily;
had she not besought him endlessly with breathless
prayer.

"Will he not? Wait a year—wait a year."

"What then?" asked Folle-Farine, with a quick
startled breath.

"In a year you will be a woman, and he always
hears women, they say."

"He hears you?"

The fair woman above laughed:

"Perhaps; in his fashion. But he pays me ill as
yet," and she plucked one of the silver pins from
her hair, and stabbed the rosy foam of the saxifrage
through and through with it; for she was but a
gardener's wife, and was restless and full of discon-
tent.

"Get you gone," she added quickly, "or I will
throw a stone at you, you witch; you have the evil
eye, they say, and you may strike me blind if you
stare so."

Folle-Farine went on her way over the sharp
stones with a heavy heart. That picture in the

casement had made that passage bright to her many a time; and when at last that picture had moved and spoken, it had only mocked her and reviled her as the rest did.

The street was dark for her like all the others now.

The gardener's wife, leaning there, with the green and gold of the vineleaves brushing her hair, looked after her down the crooked way.

"That young wretch will be more beautiful than I," she thought; and the thought was bitter to her, as such a one is to a fair woman.

Folle-Farine went slowly and sadly through the street, with her head dropped, and the large osier basket trailing behind her over the stones.

She was well used to be pelted with words hard as hailstones, and usually heeded them little, or gave them back with sullen, fierce defiance. But from this woman they had wounded her; from that bright bower of golden leaves and scarlet flowers she had faintly fancied some stray beam of light might wander even to her.

She was soon outside the gates of the town, and beyond the old walls, where the bramble and the lichen grew over the huge stones of ramparts and fortifications, useless and decayed from age.

The country roads and paths, the silver streams and the wooden bridges, the lanes through which the market mules picked their careful way, the fields in which the white-capped peasant women and the brindled oxen were at work, stretched all before her in a radiant air, sweet with the scent of ripening fruits from many orchards.

Here and there a wayside crucifix rose dark against the sun; here and there a chapel bell sounded from under some little peaked red roof. The cattle dozed beside meadow ditches that were choked with wild flowers; the dogs lay down beside their sheep and slept.

At the first cottage which she passed, the housewife sat out under a spreading chestnut tree, weaving lace upon her knee.

Folle-Farine looked wistfully at the woman, who was young and pretty, and who darted her swift skilled hand in and out and around the bobbins, keeping time meanwhile with a mirthful burden that she sang.

The woman looked up and frowned as the girl passed by her.

A little way farther on there was a winehouse by the roadside, built of wood, vine-wreathed, and half hidden in the tall flowering briars of its garden.

Out of the lattice there was leaning a maiden with the silver cross on her bosom shining in the sun, and her meek blue eyes smiling down from under the tower of her high white cap. She was reaching a carnation to a student who stood below, with long fair locks and ruddy cheeks, and a beard yellow with the amber down of twenty years; and who kissed her white wrist as he caught the red flower.

Folle-Farine glanced at the pretty picture with a dull wonder and a nameless pain: what could it mean to be happy like that?

Half a league onward she passed another cottage shadowed by a sycamore-tree, and with the swallows whirling around its tall twisted stone chimneys, and a beurré pear covering with branch and bloom its old grey walls. An aged woman sat sipping coffee in the sun, and a young one was sweeping the blue and white tiles with a broom, singing gaily as she swept.

"Art thou well placed, my mother?" she asked, pausing to look tenderly at the withered brown face, on which the shadows of the sycamore leaves were playing.

The old mother smiled, steeping her bread in the coffee-bowl.

" Surely, child ; I can feel the sun and hear you sing."

She was happy though she was blind.

Folle-Farine stood a moment and looked at them across a hedge of honeysuckle.

" How odd it must be to have anyone to care to hear your voice like that ! " she thought ; and she went on her way through the poppies and the corn, half softened, half enraged.

Was she lower than they because she could find no one to care for her or take gladness in her life ? or was she greater than they because all human delights were to her as the dead letters of an unknown tongue ?

Down a pathway fronting her which ran midway between the yellowing seas of wheat and a belt of lilac clover, and over which a swarm of bees was murmuring, there came a countrywoman, crushing the herbage under her heavy shoes, ragged, picturesque, sunbrowned, swinging deep brass pails as she went to the herds on the hillside. She carried a child twisted into the folds of her dress ; a boy, half asleep, with his curly head against her breast.

As she passed, the woman drew her kerchief over her bosom and over the brown rosy face of the child.

" She shall not look at thee, my darling," she

muttered. "Her look withered Rémy's little limb."
And she covered the child jealously, and turned
aside, so that she should tread a separate pathway
through the clover, and needed not to brush the garments of the one she was compelled to pass.

Folle-Farine heard, and laughed aloud.

She knew of what the woman was thinking.

In the summer of the previous year, as she had
passed the tanyard on the western bank of the river,
the tanner's little son, rushing out in haste, had
curled his mouth in insult at her, and clapping his
hands, hissed in a child's love of cruelty the mock-
ing words which he had heard his elders use of her.
In answer, she had only turned her head and looked
down at him with calm eyes of scorn.

But the child, running out fast, and startled by
that regard, had slipped upon a shred of leather and
had fallen heavily, breaking his left leg at the knee.

The limb, unskilfully dealt with, and enfeebled by
a tendency to disease, had never been restored, but
hung limp, crooked, useless, withered from below
the knee. Through all the country side the little
cripple, Rémy, creeping out into the sun upon his
crutches, was pointed out in a passionate pity as the
object of her sorcery, the victim of her vengeance.

When she had heard what they said she had

laughed as she laughed now, drawing together her straight brows and showing her glistening teeth.

All the momentary softness died in her now as the peasant covered the boy's face and turned aside into the clover. She laughed aloud, and swept on through the half-ripe corn with that swift, harmonious, majestic movement which was inborn in her, as it is inborn in the deer or the antelope ; singing again as she went those strange wild airs, like the sigh of the wind, which were all the language which lingered in her memory from the land that had seen her birth.

To such aversion as this she was too well used for it to be a matter of even notice to her. She knew that she was marked and shunned by the community amidst which her lot was cast; and she accepted proscription without wonder and without resistance.

Folle-Farine : the Dust. What lower thing did earth hold ?

In this old-world district, amidst the pastures and corn-lands of Normandy, superstition had taken a hold which the passage of centuries and the advent of revolution had done very little to lessen.

Few of the people could read and fewer still could write. They knew nothing but what their priests and

their politicians told them to believe. They went to
their beds with the poultry, and rose as the cock
crew : they went to mass, as their ducks to the osier
and weed ponds ; and to the conscription as their
lambs to the slaughter.

They understood that there was a world beyond
them, but they remembered it only as the best
market for their fruit, their fowls, their lace, their
skins. Their brains were as dim as were their
oil-lit streets at night; though their lives were
content and mirthful, and for the most part pious.
They went out into the summer meadows chaunting
aves, in seasons of drought to pray for rain on their
parching orchards, in the same credulity with which
they groped through the winter fog, bearing torches
and chaunting dirges to gain a blessing at seed
time on their bleak black fallows.

The beauty and the faith of the old Mediæval life
were with them still; and with its beauty and its
faith were its bigotry and its cruelty likewise.

They led simple and contented lives ; for the
most part honest, and amongst themselves cheerful
and kindly ; preserving much grace of colour, of
costume, of idiosyncracy, because apart from the
hueless communism and characterless monotony of
modern cities.

But they believed in sorcery and in devilry; they were brutal to their beasts, and could be as brutal to their foes; they were steeped in legend and tradition from their cradles; and all the darkest superstitions of dead ages still found home and treasury in their hearts and at their hearths.

Therefore, believing her a creature of evil, they were inexorable against her; and thought that in being so they did their duty.

They had always been a religious people in this birth country of the Flamma race; the strong poetic reverence of their forefathers, which had symbolised itself in the carving of every lintel, corbel, or buttress in their streets, and in the fashion of every spire on which a weather-vane could gleam against the sun, was still in their blood; the poetry had departed, but the bigotry remained.

Their ancestors had burned wizards and witches by the score in the open square of the cathedral place, and their grandsires and granddams had in brave, dumb, ignorant peasant fashion held fast to the lily and the cross, and gone by hundreds to the salutation of the axe and the baptism of the sword in the red days of revolution.

They were the same people still; industrious,

frugal, peaceful, loyal, wedded to old ways and to old relics, content on little, and serene of heart; yet, withal, where they feared or where they hated, brutal with the brutality begotten of abject ignorance. And they had been so to this outcast whom they all called Folle-Farine.

When she had first come amidst them, a little desolate foreign child, mute with the dumbness of an unknown tongue, and cast adrift amongst strange people, unfamiliar ways, and chill blank glances, she had shyly tried in a child's vague instincts of appeal and trust to make friends with the other children that she saw, and to share a little in the mothers' smiles and the babies' pastimes that were all around her in the glad green world of summer.

But she had been denied and rejected with hard words and harder blows; at her coming the smiles had changed to frowns, and the pastime into terror.

She was proud, she was shy, she was savage; she felt rather than understood that she was suspected and reviled; she ceased to seek her own kind, and only went for companionship and sympathy to the creatures of the fields and the woods, to the things of the earth and the sky and the water.

" Thou art the devil's daughter! " half in sport hissed the youths in the market-place against her as the little child went amongst them, carrying a load for her grandsire, heavier than her arms knew how to bear.

" Thou wert plague-spotted from thy birth," said the old man himself, as she strained her small limbs to and fro the floors of his storehouses, carrying wood or flour or tiles or rushes, or whatever there chanced to need such convoy.

" Get thee away, we are not to touch thee!" hissed the six-year-old infants at play by the river when she waded in amidst them to reach with her lither arms the far off water-flower which they were too timorous to pluck, and tendered it to the one who had desired it.

" The devil begot thee, and my cow fell ill yesternight after thou hadst laid hands on her!" muttered the old women, lifting a stick as she went near to their cattle in the meadows to brush off with a broad dockleaf the flies that were teasing the poor, meek, patient beasts.

So, cursed when she did her duty and driven away when she tried to do good, her young soul had hardened itself and grown fierce, mute, callous, isolated.

There were only the four-footed things, so wise, so silent, so tender of heart, so bruised of body, so innocent, and so agonised, that had compassion for her, and saved her from utter desolation. In the mild sad gaze of the cow, in the lustrous suffering eyes of the horse, in the noble frank faith of the dog, in the soft bounding glee of the lamb, in the unwearied toil of the ass, in the tender industry of the bird, she had sympathy and she had example.

She loved them and they loved her.

She saw that they were sinless, diligent, faithful, devoted, loyal servers of base masters; loving greatly, and for their love goaded, beaten, over-tasked, slaughtered.

She took the lesson to heart; and hated men and women with a bitter hatred.

So she had grown up for ten years, caring for no human thing, except in a manner for the old man Marcellin, who was, like her, proscribed.

The priests had striven to turn her soul what they had termed heavenward; but their weapons had been wrath and intimidation. She would have none of them. No efforts that they or her grandsire made had availed; she would be starved, thrashed, cursed, maltreated as they would; she could not understand their meaning, or would not submit herself to their religion.

As years went on they had found the contest
hopeless, so had abandoned her to the devil, who
had made her; and the daughter of one whom
the whole province had called saint had never
passed within church-doors or known the touch
of holy water save when they had cast it on her as
an exorcism. And when she met a priest in the
open roads or on the byepaths of the fields, she
always sang in loud defiance her wildest melodies.

Where had she learnt these?

They had been sung to her by Phratos, and
taught by him.

Who had he been?

Her old life was obscure to her memory, and yet
glorious even in that dimness.

She did not know who those people had been
with whom she had wandered, nor in what land they
had dwelt.

But that wondrous free life remained on her
remembrance as a thing never to be forgotten or
to be known again; a life odorous with bursting
fruits and budding flowers; full of strangest and
of sweetest music; spent for ever under green leaves
and suns that had no setting; for ever beside
fathomless waters and winding forests; for ever

rhymed to melody and soothed to the measure of deep winds and drifting clouds.

For she had forgotten all except its liberty and its loveliness; and the old gipsy life of the Liébana remained with her only as some stray fragment of an existence passed in another world from which she was now an exile, and revived in her only in the fierce passion of her nature, in her bitter, vague rebellion, in her longing to be free, in her anguish of vain desires for richer hues and bluer skies and wilder winds than those amidst which she toiled.

At times she remembered likewise the songs and the melodies of Phratos; remembered them when the moon rays swept across the white breadth of water lilies, or the breath of the spring stole through the awakening woods; and when she remembered them she wept—wept bitterly, where none could look on her.

She never thought of Phratos as a man; as of one who had lived in a human form, and was now lying dead in an earthly grave. Her memory of him was as of some nameless creature half divine, whose footsteps brought laughter and music, with eyes bright as a bird's, yet sad as a dog's, and a voice for ever singing; clad in goat's hair, gigantic and gay; a creature that had spoken tenderly to her, that had bidden her laugh and rejoice, that had carried her when she was weary; that had taught her to sleep under the dewy leaves, and to greet the things of the night as soft sisters, and to fear nothing in the whole living world, in the earth, or the air, or the sky, and to tell the truth though a falsehood were to save the bare feet from flintstones, and naked shoulders from the stick, and an empty body from hunger and thirst. A creature that seemed to her in her memories even as the faun seemed to the fancies of the children of the Piræus; a creature half man and half animal, glad and grotesque, full of mirth and of music, belonging to the forest, to the brook, to the stars, to the leaves, wandering like the wind, and, like the wind, homeless.

This was all her memory; but she cherished it; in the face of the priests she bent her straight black brows and curled her scornful scarlet lips, but for the sake of Phratos she held one religion; though she hated men she told them never a lie, and asked of them never alms.

She went now along the white level roads, the empty basket balanced on her head, her form moving with the free harmonious grace of desert women, and she sang as she went the old sweet songs of the broken viol.

She was friendless and desolate; she was ill-fed, she was heavily tasked; she toiled without thanks; she was ignorant of even so much knowledge as the peasants about her had; she was without a past or a future, and her present had in it but daily toil and bitter words; hunger, and thirst, and chastisement.

Yet for all that she sang;—sang because the vitality in her made her dauntless of all evil; because the abundant life opening in her made her glad in despite of fate; because the youth, and the strength, and the soul that were in her could not utterly be brutalised, could not wholly cease from feeling the gladness of the sun, the coursing of the breeze, the liberty of nature, the sweet quick sense of living.

Before long she reached the spot where the old man Marcellin was breaking his stones.

His pile was raised much higher; he sat astride on a log of timber and hammered the flints on and on, on and on, without looking up; the dust, where the tramp of the people had raised it, was still thick on the leaves and the herbage; and the prayers and the chants had failed as yet to bring the slightest cloud, the faintest rain mist across the hot unbroken azure of the skies.

Marcellin was her only friend; the proscribed always adhere to one another; when they are few they can only brood and suffer, harmlessly; when they are many they rise as with one foot and strike as with one hand. Therefore, it is always perilous to make the lists of any proscription over long.

The child, who was also an outcast, went to him and paused; in a curious, lifeless, bitter way they cared for one another; this girl who had grown to believe herself born of hell, and this man who had grown to believe that he had served hell.

With the bastard Folle-Farine and with the regicide Marcellin the people had no association, and for them no pity; therefore they had found each other by the kinship of proscription; and in a way there was love between them.

"You are glad, since you sing!" said the old man to her as she passed him again on her homeward way, and paused again beside him.

"The birds in cages sing," she answered him. "But, think you they are glad?"

"Are they not?"

She sat down a moment beside him, on the bank which was soft with moss, and odorous with wild flowers curling up the stems of the poplars and straying over into the corn beyond.

"Are they? Look. Yesterday I passed a cottage, it is on the great south road; far away from here. The house was empty; the people, no doubt, were gone to labour in the fields; there was a wicker cage hanging to the wall, and in the cage there was a blackbird. The sun beat on his head; his square of sod was a dry clod of bare earth; the heat had dried every drop of water in his pan; and yet the bird was singing. Singing how? In torment, beating his breast against the bars till the blood started, crying to the skies to have mercy on him and to let rain fall. His song was shrill; it had a scream in it; still he sang. Do you say the merle was glad?"

"What did you do?" asked the old man, still breaking his stones with a monotonous rise and fall of his hammer.

"I took the cage down and opened the door."

"And he?"

"He shot up in the air first, then dropped down amidst the grasses, where a little brook which the drought had not dried, was still running; and he bathed and drank and bathed again, seeming mad with the joy of the water. When I lost him from sight he was swaying among the leaves on a bough over the river; but then he was silent."

"And what do you mean by that?"

Her eyes clouded; she was mute. She vaguely knew the meaning it bore to herself, but it was beyond her to express it. All things of nature had voices and parables for her, because her fancy was vivid and her mind was dreamy; but that mind was still too dark, and too profoundly ignorant, for her to be able to shape her thoughts into metaphor or deduction.

The bird had spoken to her; by his silence as by his song; but what he had uttered she could not well utter again. Save, indeed, that song was not gladness, and neither was silence pain.

Marcellin, although he had asked her, had asked needlessly; for he also knew.

"And what, think you, the people said when they went back and found the cage empty?" he pursued, still echoing his words and hers by the ringing sound of the falling hammer.

A smile curled her lips.

"That was no thought of mine," she said carelessly. "They had done wickedly to cage him; to set him free I would have pulled down their thatch, or stove in their door, had need been."

"Good!" said the old man briefly, with a gleam of light over his harsh lean face.

He looked up at her as he worked, the shivered flints flying right and left.

"It was a pity to make you a woman," he muttered, as his keen gaze swept over her.

"A woman!" She echoed the words dully and half wonderingly; she could not understand it in connection with herself.

A woman; that was a woman who sat in the sun under the fig tree, working her lace on a frame; that was a woman who leaned out of her lattice tossing a red carnation to her lover; that was a woman who swept the open porch of her house, singing as she cleared the dust away; that was a woman who strode on her blithe way through the clover, carrying her child at her breast.

She seemed to have no likeness to them, no kindred with them; she, a beast of burden, a creature soulless and homeless; an animal made to fetch and carry, to be cursed and beaten, to know neither love nor hope, neither past nor future, but only a certain dull patience and furious hate, a certain dim pleasure in labour and indifference to pain.

"It was a pity to make you a woman," said the old man once more. "You might be a man worth something; but a woman!—a thing that has no

medium ; no haven between hell and heaven ; no
option save to sit by the hearth to watch the pot
boil and suckle the children, or to go out into
the streets and the taverns to mock at men and to
murder them. Which will you do in the
future ?"

"What ?"

She scarcely knew the meaning of the word.
She saw that the female creatures round her
were of all shades of age, from the young girls
with their peach-like cheeks to the old crones brown
and withered as last year's nuts; she knew that if
she lived on she would be old likewise; but of a
future she had no conception, no ideal. She had
been left too ignorant to have visions of any other
world hereafter than this one which the low-lying
green hills and the arc of the pale blue sky shut in
upon her.

She had one desire, indeed—a desire vague yet
fierce—the desire for liberty. But it was such
desire as the bird which she had freed had known ;
the desire of instinct, the desire of existence, only ;
her mind was powerless to conceive a future,
because a future is a hope, and of hope she knew
nothing.

The old man glanced at her, and saw that she

had not comprehended. He smiled with a certain bitter pity.

"I spoke idly," he said to himself; "slaves cannot have a future. But yet—"

Yet he saw that the creature who was so ignorant of her own powers, of her own splendours, of her own possibilities, had even now a beauty as great as that of a lustrous eastern-eyed passion flower ; and he knew that to a woman who has such beauty as this the world holds out in its hand the tender of at least one future—one election, one kingdom, one destiny.

"Women are loved," she said, suddenly; "will any one love me ?"

Marcellin smiled bitterly.

"Many will love you, doubtless—as the wasp loves the peach that he kisses with his sting, and leaves rotten to drop from the stem !"

She was silent again, revolving his meaning; it lay beyond her, both in the peril which it embodied from others, and the beauty in herself which it implied. She could reach no conception of herself, save as what she now was, a body servant of toil, a beast of burden like a young mule.

"But all shun me, as even the wasp shuns the bitter oak apple," she said, slowly and dreamily;

" who should love me, even as the wasp loves the peach ? "

Marcellin smiled his grim and shadowy smile. He made answer—

" Wait ! "

She sat mute once more, revolving this strange, brief word in her thoughts—strange to her, with a promise as vague, as splendid, and as incomprehensible as the prophecy of empire to a slave.

" The future ? " she said, at last. " That means something that one has not, and that is to come—is it so ? "

" Something that one never has, and that never comes," muttered the old man, wearily cracking the flints in two ; " something that one possesses in one's sleep, and that is farther off each time that one awakes; and yet a thing that one sees always— sees even when one lies a-dying, they say—for men are fools."

Folle-Farine listened, musing, with her hands clasped on the handle of her empty basket, and her chin resting upon them, and her eyes watching a maimed butterfly drag its wings of emerald and diamond through the hot, pale, sickly dust.

" I dream ! " she said, suddenly, as she stooped

and lifted the wounded insect gently on to the edge of a leaf. " But I dream wide awake."

Marcellin smiled.

" Never say so. They will think you mad. That is only what foolish things, called poets, do."

" What is a poet ? "

" A foolish thing, I tell you—mad enough to believe that men will care to strain their eyes, as he strains his, to see the face of a God who never looks and never listens."

"Ah ! "

She was so accustomed to be told, that all she did was unlike to others, and was either wicked or was senseless, that she saw nothing except the simple statement of a fact in the rebuke which he had given her. She sat quiet, gazing down into the thick white dust of the road, bestirred by the many feet of mules and men that had trodden through it since the dawn.

" I dream beautiful things," she pursued, slowly. " In the moonlight most often. I seem to remember, when I dream—so much ! so much ! "

" Remember — what should you remember ? You were but a baby when they brought you hither."

" So they say. But I might live before, in my

father's kingdom. In the devil's kingdom? Why not?"

"Why not, indeed! Perhaps we all lived there once; and that is why we all, through all our lives, hanker to get back to it!"

"I ask him so often to take me back, but he does not seem ever to hear."

"Chut! He will hear in his own good time. The devil never passes by a woman."

"A woman!" she repeated. The word seemed to have no likeness and no fitness with herself.

A woman—she!—a creature made to be beaten, and sworn at, and shunned, and loaded like a mule, and driven like a bullock!

"Look you," said the old man, resting his hammer for a moment, and wiping the sweat from his brow. "I have lived in this vile place forty years. I remember the woman that they say bore you —Reine Flamma. She was a beautiful woman, and pure as snow, and noble, and innocent. She wearied God incessantly. I have seen her stretched for hours at the foot of that cross. She was wretched; and she entreated her God to take away her monotonous misery, and to give her some life new and fair. But God never answered. He left her to herself. It was the devil that heard—and replied."

"Then, is the devil juster than their God?"

Marcellin leaned his hammer on his knee, and his voice rose clear and strong; as it had rung of yore from the Tribune.

"He looks so, at the least. It is his wisdom, and that is why his following is so large. Nay, I say, when God is deaf the devil listens.

"That is his wisdom, see you.

"So often the poor little weak human soul, striving to find the right way, cries feebly for help, and none answer.

"The poor little weak soul is blind and astray in the busy streets of the world.

"It lifts its voice, but its voice is so young and so feeble, like the pipe of a newly-born bird in the dawn, that it is drowned in the shouts and the manifold sounds of those hard, crowded, cruel streets, where every one is for himself, and no man has ears for his neighbour. It is hungered, it is athirst, it is sorrowful, it is blinded, it is perplexed, it is afraid.

"It cries often, but God and man leave it to itself.

"Then the devil, who hearkens always, and

who, though all the trumpets blowing their brazen music in the streets bray in his honour, yet is too wise to lose even the slightest sound of any in distress—since of such are the largest sheaves of his harvest—comes to the little soul, and teaches it with tenderness, and guides it towards the paths of gladness, and fills its lips with the bread of sweet passions, and its nostrils with the savour of fair vanities, and blows in its ear the empty breath of men's lungs, till that sickly wind seems divinest music.

" Then is the little soul dazzled and captured, and made the devil's for evermore ; half through its innocence, half through its weakness ; but chiefly of all because God and man would not hear its cries whilst yet it was sinless and only astray."

He ceased, and the strokes of his hammer rang again on the sharp flint stones.

She had listened with her lips parted breathlessly, and her night-like eyes dilated. In the years of his youth the old man had possessed that rare power which can tip words with fire, and send them burning and keen into the coldest heart ; and the power was still there, when it woke up from the stupor of a life of toil, and the silence of a harsh old age. In the far distant time, when

he had been amidst the world of men, he had
known how to utter the words that charmed to
stillness a raging multitude. He had not altogether lost this eloquence at such rare times as he
still cared to break his silence, and to unfold the unforgotten memories of a life long dead.

He would speak thus to her, but to no
other.

Folle-Farine listened, mute and breathless, her
eyes uplifted to the sun, where it was sinking
westward through a pomp of golden and of purple
cloud. He was the only creature who ever spoke
to her as though she likewise were human ; and she
followed his words with dumb unquestioning faith,
as a dog its master's footsteps.

" The soul! What is the soul ? " she muttered,
at length.

He caught in his hand the beautiful diamond-
winged butterfly, which now, freed of the dust and
drinking in the sunlight, was poised on a fox-
glove in the hedge growing near him, and held it
against the light.

" What is it that moves this creature's wings, and
glances in its eyes, and gives it delight in the summer's warmth, in the orchid's honey, and in the
lime-tree's leaves ?

N 2

"I do not know; but I know that I can kill it—with one grind of my heel.

"So much we know of the soul—no more."

She freed it from his hand.

"Whoever made it, then, was cruel. If he could give it so much power, why not have given it a little more, so that it could escape you always?"

"You ask what men have asked ten times ten thousand years—since the world began—without an answer. Because the law of all creation is cruelty, I suppose; because the dust of death is always the breath of life. The great man, dead, changes to a million worms, and lives again in the juices of the grass above his grave. It matters little. The worms destroy; the grasses nourish. Few great men do more than the first, or as much as the last."

"But get you homeward," he continued, breaking off his parable; "it is two hours past noon, and if you be late on the way you pay for it with your body. Begone."

She nodded her head, and went; he seldom used gentle words to her, and yet she knew, in a way, that he cared for her; moreover, she rejoiced in that bitter, caustic contempt in which he, the oldest man amidst them, held all men.

His words were the only thing that had aroused
her dulled brain to its natural faculties; in a manner, from him she had caught something of knowledge—something, too, of intellect; he alone pre-
vented her from sinking to that absolute unquestioning despair which surely ends in idiotcy or in
self-murder.

She pursued her way in silence across the fields,
and along the straight white road, and across a
wooden bridge that spanned the river, to her
home.

There was a gentler lustre in her eyes, and her
mouth had the faint light of a half smile upon it;
she did not know what hope meant; it never seemed
possible to her that her fate could be other than it
was, since so long the messengers and emissaries of
her father's empire had been silent and leaden-
footed to her call.

Yet, in a manner, she was comforted, for had not
two mouths that day bidden her " wait " ?

She entered at length the little wood of Yprés,
`and heard that rush and music of the deep mill
water, which was the sole thing she had learned to
love in all the place.

Beyond it were the apple orchards and fruit
gardens which rendered Claudis Flamma back full

recompense for all the toil they cost him—recompense so large, indeed, that many disbelieved in that poverty which he was wont to aver weighed so hardly and so tightly on him. Both were now rich in all their mature abundance, since the stream which rushed through them had saved them from the evil effects of the long drought so severely felt in other districts. The cherry trees were scarlet with their latest fruit; the great pumpkins glowed amongst their leaves in tawny orange heaps; little russet-breasted bullfinches beat their wings vainly at the fine network that enshrouded the paler gold of the wall apricots; a grey cat was stealing amongst the delicate yellows of the pear-shaped marrows; where a round green wrinkled melon lay a-ripening in the sun, a gorgeous dragon-fly was hovering, and a mother-mavis, in her simple coif of brown and white and grey, was singing with all the gladness of her sunny summer joys.

Beyond a hedge of prickly thorn the narrower flower garden stretched, spanned by low stone walls, made venerable by the silvery beards of lichens; and the whole earth was full of colour from the crimson and the golden gladioli; from the carmine-hued carnations; from the deep-blue lupins, and the Gloire de Dijon roses ; from the green slender stems, and the pure white cups, of the virginal lilies ; and from the gorgeous beetles, with their purple tunics and their shields of bronze, like Grecian hoplites in battle array. While everywhere, above this sweet glad garden world, the butterflies, purple and jewelled, the redstarts in their ruby coats, the dainty azure-winged blue-warblers, the golden-girdled wasp with his pinions light as mist, and the velvet-coated bee with his pleasant harvest song, flew ever in the sunlight, murmuring, poising, praising, rejoicing.

The place was beautiful in its own simple, quiet way; lying in a hollow, where the river tumbled down in two or three short breaks and leaps which broke its habitual smooth and sluggish form, and brought it in a sheet of dark water and with a million foam-bells against the walls of the mill-house and under the ponderous wheels.

The wooden house itself also was picturesque, in the old fashion common when men built their dwellings slowly and for love ; with all its countless carvings black by age, its jutting beams shapen into grotesque human likeness and tragic masks ; its parquetted work run over by the green cups of stoneworts, and its high roof with deep shelving eaves bright with diapered tiles of blue and white and rose, and alive all day with curling swallows, with pluming pigeons, with cooing doves.

It was beautiful; and the heart of Reine Flamma's young daughter doubtless would have clung to it, with all a child's instinct of love and loyalty to its home, had it not been to her only a prison-house wherein three bitter gaolers for ever ruled her with a rod of iron—bigotry and penury and cruelty.

She flung herself down a moment in the garden, on the long grass under a mulberry tree, ere she went in to give her account of the fruit sold and the monies brought by her.

She had been on foot since four o'clock in the dawn of that sultry day; her only meal had been a bowl of cold milk and a hunch of dry bread crushed in her strong small teeth. She always toiled hard at such bodily labour as was set to her; to domestic work, to the work of the distaff and spindle, of the stove and the needle, they had never been able to break her; they had found that she would be beaten black and blue ere she would be bound to it; but against open air exertion she had never rebelled, and she had in her all the strength and the swiftness of the nomadic

race of the Liébana, and had nought of their indolence and their dishonesty.

She was very hungry, she was again thirsty; yet
she did not break off a fruit from any bough about
her ;· she did not steep her hot lips in any one of
the cool juicy apricots which studded the stones of
the wall beyond her.

No one had ever taught her honesty, except indeed in that dim dead time when Phratos had
closed her small hands in his whenever they
had stretched out to some forbidden thing, and
had said, " Take the goods the gods give thee,
but steal not from men." And yet honest she was,
by reason of the fierce proud savage independence
in her, and her dim memories of that sole friend
loved and lost.

She wanted many a thing, many a time ;—nay,
nearly every hour that she lived, she wanted those
sheer necessaries which make life endurable ; but
she had taught herself to do without them rather
than owe them by prayer or by plunder to that
human race which she hated, and to which she
always doubted her own kinship.

Buried in the grass, she now abandoned herself
to the bodily delights of rest, of shade, of coolness,
of sweet odours : the scent of the fruits and flowers

was heavy on the air; the fall of the water made a
familiar tempestuous music on her ear; and her
fancy, poetic still, though deadened by a life of
ignorance and toil, was stirred by the tender tones
of the numberless birds that sang about her.

"The earth and the air are good," she thought,
as she lay there watching the dark leaves sway
in the foam and the wind, and the bright-bosomed
birds float from blossom to blossom.

For there was latent in her, all untaught, that
old pantheistic instinct of the divine age, when
the world was young, to behold a sentient consciousness in every leaf unfolded to the light; to
see a soul in every created thing the day shines
on; to feel the presence of an eternal life in every
breeze that moves, in every grass that grows; in
every flame that lifts itself to heaven; in every
bell that vibrates on the air; in every moth that
soars to reach the stars.

Pantheism is the religion of the poet; and nature
had made her a poet, though man as yet had but
made of her an outcast, a slave, and a beast of
burden.

"The earth and the air are good," she thought,
watching the sun-rays pierce the purple heart of a
passion-flower, the shadows move across the deep

brown water, the radiant butterfly alight upon a lily, the scarlet-throated birds dart in and out, through the yellow feathery blossoms of the limes.

All birds were her friends.

Phratos had taught her in her infancy many notes of their various songs, and many ways and means of luring them to come and rest upon her shoulder and peck the berries in her hand. She had lived so much in the open fields and amongst the woods that she had made her chief companions of them. She could emulate so deftly all their voices, from the call of the wood dove to the chant of the blackbird, and from the trill of the nightingale to the twitter of the titmouse, that she could summon them all to her at will, and have dozens of them fluttering around her head and swaying their pretty bodies on her wrist.

It was one of her ways that seemed to the peasantry so weird and magical; and they would come home from their fields on a spring day-break and tell their wives in horror how they had seen the devil's daughter in the red flush of the sunrise, ankle-deep in violets, and covered with birds from head to foot, hearing their whispers, and giving them her messages to carry in return.

One meek-eyed woman had dared once to say

that St. Francis had done as much, and it had been accredited to him as a fair action and virtuous knowledge; but she was frowned down and chattered down by her louder neighbours, who told her that she might look for some sharp judgment of heaven for daring to couple together the blessed name of the holy saint and the accursed name of this foul spirit.

But all they could say could not break the charmed communion between Folle-Farine and her feathered comrades.

She loved them and they her. In the hard winter she had always saved some of her scanty meal for them, and in the springtime and the summer they always rewarded her with floods of songs and soft caresses from their nestling wings.

There were no rare birds, no birds of moor and mountain, in that cultivated and populous district; but to her all the little home-bred things of pasture and orchard were full of poetry and of character.

The robins, with that pretty air of boldness with which they veil their real shyness and timidity; the strong and saucy sparrows, powerful by the strength of all mediocrities and majorities; all the dainty families of finches in their gay apparellings ; the plain brown bird that filled the night with music ; the gorgeous oriole ruffling in gold, the gilded princeling of them all ; the little blue warblers, the violets of the air ; the kingfishers who had hovered so long over the forget-me-nots upon the rivers that they had caught the colours of the flowers on their wings ; the bright black-caps green as the leaves, with their yellow waist-coats and velvet hoods, the innocent freebooters of the woodland liberties : all these were her friends and lovers, various as any human crowds of court or city.

She loved them ; they and the fourfooted beasts were the sole things that did not flee from her ; and the woeful and mad slaughter of them by the peasants was to her a grief passionate in its despair. She did not reason on what she felt ; but to her a bird slain was a trust betrayed, an inno-cence defiled, a creature of heaven struck to earth.

Suddenly on the silence of the garden there was a little shrill sound of pain ; the birds flew high in air, screaming and startled ; the leaves of a bough of ivy shook as with a struggle.

She rose and looked ; a line of twine was trembling against the foliage ; in its noosed end the throat

of the mavis had been caught; it hung trembling
and clutching at the air convulsively with its little
drawn up feet. It had flown into the trap as it
had ended its joyous song and soared up to join
its brethren.

There were a score of such traps set, in the
miller's garden.

She unloosed the cord from about its tiny neck,
set it free, and laid it down upon the ivy : the
succour came too late ; the little gentle body
was already without breath ; the feet had ceased
to beat the air; the small soft head had drooped
feebly on one side ; the lifeless eyes had started
from their sockets ; the throat was without song for
evermore.

" The earth would be good but for men," she
thought, as she stood with the little dead bird in
her hand.

Its mate, which was poised on a rose bough, flew
straight to it, and curled round and round about
the small slain body, and piteously bewailed its
fate, and mourned, refusing to be comforted,
agitating the air with trembling wings, and giving
out vain cries of grief.

Vain ; for the little joyous life was gone ; the life
that asked only of God and Man a home in the

green leaves; a drop of dew from the cup of a
rose; a bough to swing on in the sunlight; a
summer day to celebrate in song.

All the winter through, it had borne cold and
hunger and pain without lament; it had saved
the soil from destroying larvæ, and purified the
trees from all foul germs; it had built its little
home unaided, and had fed its nestlings without
alms; it had given its sweet song lavishly to the
winds, to the blossoms, to the empty air, to the
deaf ears of men; and now it lay dead in its
innocence; trapped and slain because a human
greed begrudged it a berry worth the thousandth
part of a copper coin.

Out from the porch of the mill-house Claudis
Flamma came, with a knife in his hand and a
basket, to cut lilies for one of the choristers of the
cathedral, since the morrow would be the religious
feast of the Visitation of Mary.

He saw the dead thrush in her hand, and
chuckled to himself as he went by.

" The tenth bird trapped since sunrise," he
said, thinking how shrewd and how sure in their
make were these traps of twine that he set in
the grass and the leaves.

She said nothing; but the darkness of disgust

swept over her face, as he came in sight in the distance.

She knelt down and scraped a hole in the earth; and laid moss in it and put the mavis softly on its green and fragrant bier, and covered it with handsful of fallen rose leaves and with a sprig or two of thyme.

Around her head the widowed thrush flew ceaselessly, uttering sad cries;—who now should wander with him through the sunlight?—who now should rove with him above the blossoming fields?—who now should sit with him beneath the boughs hearing the sweet rain fall between the leaves? —who now should wake with him whilst yet the world was dark, to feel the dawn break, ere the east were red, and sing a welcome to the unborn day?

CHAPTER IV.

MEANWHILE Claudis Flamma cut the lilies for the cathedral altars, muttering many holy prayers as he gathered the flowers of Mary.

When the white lily sheaves had been borne away, kept fresh in wet moss, by the young chorister who had been sent for them, the miller turned to her.

" Where is the money ? "

She, standing beside the buried bird, undid the leathern thong about her waist, opened the pouch, and counted out the coins, one by one, on the flat stone of a water tank amongst the lilies and the ivy.

There were a few silver pieces of slight value and some dozens of copper ones. The fruit had been left at various stalls and houses in small portions, for it was the custom to supply it fresh each day.

He caught them up with avidity, bit and tested each, counted them again and again, and yet again; after the third enumeration he turned sharply on her:

" There are two pieces too little : what have you done with them ? "

" There are two sous short," she answered him curtly. " Twelve of the figs for the tanner Florian were rotten."

" Rotten !—they were but over ripe."

" It is the same thing."

" You dare to answer me ?—animal ! I say they had only tasted a little too much of the sun. It only made them the sweeter."

" They were rotten."

" They were not. You dare to speak ! If they had been rotten, they lay under the others; he could not have seen———"

" I saw."

" You saw ! Who are you ?—a beggar—a beast— a foul offspring of sin. You dared to show them to him, I will warrant ? "

" I showed him that they were not good."

" And gave him back the two sous ? "

"I took seven sous for what were good. I took nothing for the rotten ones."

"Wretch! you dare to tell me that!"

A smile careless and sarcastic curled her mouth; her eyes looked at him with all their boldest, fiercest lustre.

"I never steal—not even from you, good Flamma."

"You have stolen now!" he shrieked, his thin and feeble voice rising in fury at his lost coins and his discovered treachery. "It is a lie that the figs were rotten; it is a lie that you took but seven sous. You stole the two sous to buy you bread and honey in the streets, or to get a drink at the wine shops. I know you; I know you; it is a devil's device to please your gluttonous appetite. The figs rotten!—not so rotten as is your soul would they be though they were black as night and though they stank as river mud! Go back to Denis Florian and bring me the two sous, or I will thrash you as a thief."

She laughed a hard, scornful, reckless laughter.

"You can thrash me; you cannot make me a thief."

"You will not go back to Florian?"

"I will not ask him to pay for what was bad."

"You will not confess that you stole the money?"

"I should lie if I did."

"Then strip."

She set her teeth in silence; and without a moment's hesitation unloosened the woollen sash knotted round her waist, and pushed down the coarse linen tunic from about her throat.

The white folds fell from off the perfect curves of her brown arms, and left bare her shining shoulders, beautiful as any sculptured Psyche's.

She was not conscious of degradation in her punishment; she had been bidden to bow her head and endure the lash from the earliest years she could remember. According to the only creed she knew, silence and fortitude and strength were the greatest of all the virtues.

She stood now in the cross lights among the lilies as she had stood when a little child, erect, unquailing, and ready to suffer; insensible of humiliation because unconscious of sin; and so tutored by severity and exposure that she had as yet none of the shy shame and the fugitive shrinking of her sex. She had only the boldness to bear, the courage to be silent, which she had had when she had stood amongst the same tall lilies, in the same summer radiance, in the years of her helpless infancy.

She uncovered herself to the lash as a brave hound crouches to it; not from inborn cowardice, but simply from the habit of obedience and of endurance.

He had used her as the Greeks the Helots; he always beat her, when she was in fault, to teach her to be faultless; and, when without offence, beat her to remind her that she was the offspring of humiliation, and a slave.

He took, as he had taken in an earlier time, a thick rope which lay coiled upon the turf ready for the binding of some straying boughs; and struck her with it, slowly. His arm had lost somewhat of its strength, and his power was unequal to his will. Still rage for the loss of his copper pieces, and the sense that she had discovered the fraudulent intention of his small knavery, lent force to his feebleness; as the scourge whistled through the air and descended on her shoulders it left bruised swollen marks to stamp its passage, and curling, adder-like, bit and drew blood.

Yet to the end she stood mute and motionless, as she had stood in her childhood; not a

nerve quivered, not a limb flinched; the colour
rushed over her bent face and her bare chest, but
she never made a movement; she never gave a
sound.

When his arm dropped from sheer exhaustion,
she still said not one word; she drew tight once
more the sash about her waist, and fastened afresh
the linen of her bodice.

The bruised and wounded flesh smarted and
ached and throbbed; but she was used to such
pain, and bore it as their wounds were borne by
the women of the Spartan games.

"Your two sous have brought you bitterness," he
muttered with a smile. "You will scarce find my
fruit rotten again in haste. There are bread and
beans within; go get a meal; I want the mule to
take flour to Barbizène."

She did not go within to eat; the bruises and
the burning of her skin made her feel sick and
weak. She went away and cast herself at full length
in the shade of the long grasses of the orchard;
resting her chin upon her hands, cooling her aching
breast against the soft damp moss; thinking,
thinking, thinking, of what she hardly knew,
except indeed that she wished that she were dead,
like the bird she had covered with the rose leaves.

He did not leave her long to even so much peace as this; his shrill voice soon called her from her rest; he bade her get ready the mule and go.

She obeyed.

The animal was saddled with his wooden pack; as many sacks as he could carry were piled upon the framework; she put her hand upon his bridle, and set out to walk to Barbizène, which was two leagues away.

"Work is the only thing to drive the devil that begat her out of her," muttered the miller, as he watched the old mule pace down the narrow tree-shadowed road that led across the fields : and he believed that he did rightly in this treatment of her.

It gratified the sharp hard cruelty of temper in him, indeed, but he did not think that in such self-indulgence he ever erred. He was a bitter, cunning, miserly old man, whose solitary tenderness of feeling and honesty of pride had been rooted out for ever when he had learned the dishonour of the woman whom he had deemed a saint. In the ten years of time which had passed since first the little brown large-eyed child had been sent to seek asylum with him,

he had grown harder and keener and more severe
with each day that rose.

Her presence was abhorrent to him, though he
kept her, partly from a savage sense of duty,
partly from the persuasion that she had the
power in her to make the strongest and the
cheapest slave he had ever owned. For the rest,
he sincerely and devoutly believed that the devil,
in some witchery of human guise, had polluted
his daughter's body and soul, and that it was by
the foul fiend and by no earthly lover that she had
conceived and borne the creature who now abode
with him.

Perhaps, also, as was but natural, he sometime
felt more furious against this offspring of hell
because ever and again some gleam of fantastic
inborn honour, some strange savage instinct of
honesty, would awake in her and oppose him, and
make him ashamed of those small and secret sins
of chicanery wherein his soul delighted, and for
which he compounded with his gods.

He had left her mind a blank, because he
thought the body laboured hardest when the brain
was still asleep, which is true ; she could not read ;
she could not write ; she knew absolutely nothing.

Yet there was a soul awake in her ; there were

innumerable thoughts and dreams brooding in her fathomless eyes; there was a desire in her, fierce and unslaked, for some other life than this life of the packhorse and of the day labourer which alone she knew.

He had done his best to degrade and to brutalise her, and in much he had succeeded; but he had not succeeded wholly. There was a liberty in her that escaped his thraldom; there was a soul in her that resisted the deadening influence of her existence.

She had none of the shame of her sex; she had none of the timorous instincts of womanhood. She had a savage stubborn courage, and she was insensible of the daily outrages of her life. She would strip bare to his word obediently, feeling only that it would be feeble and worthless to dread the pain of the lash. She would bathe in the woodland pool, remembering no more that she might be watched by human eyes than does the young tigress that has never beheld the face of man.

In all this she was brutalised and degraded by her tyrant's bondage: in other things she was far higher than he, and escaped him.

Stupified as her mind might be by the exhaustion of severe physical labour, it had still irony and it had still imagination; and under the hottest heats of temptation there were two things which by sheer instinct she resisted, and resisted so that neither of them had ever been forced on her— they were falsehood and fear.

"It is the infamous strength of the devil!" said Claudis Flamma, when he found that he could not force her to deviate from the truth.

The world says the same of those who will not feed it with lies.

CHAPTER V.

HAT long dry summer was followed by an autumn of drought and scarcity.

The prayers of the priests and peoples failed to bring down rain. The wooden Christs gazed all day long on parching lands and panting cattle. Even the broad deep rivers shrank and left their banks to bake and stink in the long drought.

The orchards sickened for lack of moisture, and the peasants went about with feverish faces, ague-stricken limbs, and trembling hearts. The corn yielded ill in the hard scorched ground, and when the winter came it was a time of dire scarcity and distress.

Claudis Flamma and a few others like him alone prospered.

The mill-house at Yprès served many purposes.

It was a granary, a market, a baker's shop, an usurer's den, all in one.

It looked a simple and innocent place. In the summer time it was peaceful and lovely, green and dark and still, with the blue sky above it, and the songs of birds all around; with its old black timbers, and its many-coloured orchards, and its pretty leafy gardens, and its grey walls washed by the hurrying stream. But in the winter it was very dreary, utterly lonely. The water roared, and the leafless trees groaned in the wind, and the great leaden clouds of rain or fog enveloped it duskily.

To the starving, wet, and woe-begone peasants who would go to it with aching bones and aching hearts, it seemed desolate and terrible. They dreaded with a great dread the sharp voice of its master—the hardest and the shrewdest and the closest fisted Norman of them all.

For they were most of them his debtors, and so were in a bitter subjugation to him, and had to pay those debts as best they might with their labour or their suffering; with the best of all their wool, or oil, or fruit; often with the last bit of silver that had been an heirloom for five centuries, or with the last bit of money buried away in an old pitcher under their apple tree to be the nest egg of their little pet daughter's dowry.

And yet Claudis Flamma was respected among them; for he could outwit them, and was believed to be very wealthy, and was a man who stood well with the good saints and with holy Church :— a wise man, in a word, with whom these northern folks had the kinship of mutual industry and avarice.

For the most part the population around Yprès was thrifty and thriving in a cautious, patient, certain way of well-doing; and, by this portion of it, the silent old miser was much honoured as a man laborious and penurious, who chose to live on a leek and a rye loaf, but who must have, it was well known, put by large gains in the thatch of his roof or under the bricks of his kitchen.

By the smaller section of it—poor, unthrifty, loose-handed fools — who belied the province of their birth so far as to be quick to spend and slow to save, and who therefore fell into want and famine and had to borrow of others their children's bread, the old miller was hated with a hate deeper and stronger because forced to be mute, and to sub mit, to cringe, and to be trod upon, in the miserable servitude of the hopeless debtor.

In the hard winter which followed on that sickly autumn these and their like fell farther in the mire of poverty than ever, and had to come and beg of Flamma loans of the commonest necessaries of their bare living. They knew that they would have to pay a hundredfold in horrible extortion when the spring and summer should bring them work, and give them fruit on their trees and crops on their little fields; but they could do no better.

It had been for many years the custom to go to Flamma in such need; and being never quit of his hold, his debtors never could try for aid elsewhere.

The weather towards the season of Noel became frightfully severe; the mill stream never stopped, but all around it was frozen, and the swamped pastures were sheets of ice. The birds died by thousands in the open country, and several of the sheep perished in snow storms on the higher lands.

There was dire want in many of the hovels and homesteads, and the bare harvests of a district, usually so opulent in the riches of the soil, brought trouble and dearth in their train.

Sickness prevailed because the old people and the children in their hunger ate berries and roots unfit for human food ; the waters swelled, the ice melted, and many homes were flooded, and some even swept away.

Old Pitchou and Claudis Flamma alone were content ; the mill wheel never stopped work, and famine prices could be asked in this extremity.

Folle-Farine worked all that winter, day after day, month after month, with scarcely a word being spoken to her, or scarcely an hour being left her that she could claim as her own.

She looked against the snow as strangely as a scarlet rose blossoming in frost there could have done ; but the people that came to and fro, even the young men amongst them, were too used to that dark vivid silent face of hers, and those lithe brown limbs that had the supple play and the golden glow of the East in them, to notice them as any loveliness : and if they did note them on some rare time, thought of them only as the marks of a vagrant and accursed race.

She was so unlike to themselves that the northern peasantry never dreamed of seeing beauty in her ; they turned their heads away when she went by, striding after her mule or bearing her pitcher from the well with the free and vigorous grace of a mountain or desert-born creature.

The sheepskin girt about her loins, the red kerchief knotted to her head, the loose lithe movements of her beautiful limbs, the sullen fire and fierce dreams in her musing eyes—all these were so unlike themselves that they saw nothing in them except what was awful or unlovely.

Half the winter went by without a kind word to her from any one except such as in that time of suffering and scarcity Marcellin spoke to her. So had every winter gone since she had come there— a time so long ago that the memory of Phratos had become so dim to her that she often doubted if he also were not a mere shadow of a dream like all the rest.

Half the winter she fared hardly and ate sparingly, and did the work of the mule and the bullocks: indifferent and knowing no better, and only staring at the stars when they throbbed in the black skies on a frosty night, and wondering if she would ever go to them, or if they would ever come to her—those splendid and familiar yet unknown things that looked on all the misery of the earth, and shone on tranquilly and did not seem to care.

Time came close on to the new year, and the distress and the cold were together at their height.

The weather was terrible; and the poor suffered immeasurably.

A score of times a-day she heard them ask bread at the mill, and a score of times saw them given a stone; she saw them come in the raw fog, pinched and shivering, and sick with ague, and she saw her grandsire deny them with a grating sarcasm or two, or take from them fifty times its value for some niggard grant of food.

" Why should I think of it, why should I care ? " she said to herself; and yet she did both, and could not help it.

There was among the sufferers one old and poor, who lived not far from the mill, by name Manon Dax.

She was a little old hardy brown woman, shrivelled and bent, yet strong, with bright eyes like a robin's, and a tough frame, eighty years old.

She had been southern born, and the wife of a stone cutter; he had been dead fifty years, and she had seen all her sons and daughters and their offspring die too ; and had now, left on her hand to rear, four young great - grandchildren, almost infants, who were always crying to her for food as new-born birds cry in their nests.

She washed a little, when she could get any linen

to wash, and she span, and she picked up the acorns and the nuts, and she tilled a small plot of ground that belonged to her hut, and she grew cabbages and potatoes and herbs on it, and so kept a roof over her head, and fed her four nestlings, and trotted to and fro in her wooden shoes all day long, and worked in hail and rain, in drought and tempest, and never complained, but said that God was good to her.

She was anxious about the children, knowing she could not live long—that was all. But then she felt sure that the Mother of God would take care of them, and so was cheerful; and did what the day brought her to do, and was content.

Now on Manon Dax, as on thousands of others, the unusual severity of the winter fell like a knife.

She was only one amongst thousands. Nobody noticed her; still it was hard.

All the springs near her dwelling were frozen for many weeks; there was no well nearer than half a league; and half a league out and half a league back every day over ground sharp and slippery with ice, with two heavy pails to carry, is not a little when one is over eighty, and has only a wisp of woollen serge between the wind and one's withered limbs.

The acorns and horse-chestnuts had all been disputed with her fiercely by boys rough and swift, who foresaw a time coming in which their pigs would be ill-fed. The roots in her little garden plot were all black and killed by the cold. The nettles had been all gathered and stewed and eaten.

The snow drove in through a big hole in her roof. The woods were ransacked for every bramble and broken bough by reivers younger and more agile than herself; she had nothing to eat, nothing to burn.

The children lay in their little beds of hay and cried all day long for food, and she had none to give them.

" If it were only myself!" she thought, stopping her ears not to hear them; if it had been only herself it would have been so easy to creep away into the corner among the dry grass, and to lie still till the cold froze the pains of hunger and made them quiet; and to feel numb and tired, and yet glad that it was all over, and to murmur that God was good, and so to let death come—content.

But it was not only herself.

The poor are seldom so fortunate—they themselves would say so unhappy—as to be alone in their homes.

There were the four small lives left to her by the poor dead foolish things she had loved,— small lives that had been rosy even-on so much hunger, and blithe even amidst so much cold ; that had been mirthful even at the flooding of the snowdrift, and happy even over a meal of mouldy crusts, or of hips and haws from the hedges.   Had been—until now, when even so much as this could not be got, and when their beds of hay were soaked through with snow-water; now—when they were quite silent, except when they sobbed out a cry for bread.

" I am eighty-two years old, and I have never since I was born asked man or woman for help, or owed man or woman a copper coin," she thought, sitting by her black hearth, across which the howling wind drove, and stopping her ears to shut out the children's cries.

She had often known severe winters, scanty food, bitter living,—she had scores of times in her long years been as famished as this, and as cold, and her house had been as desolate.

Yet she had borne it all and never asked for an alms, being strong and ignorant, and being also in fear of the world, and holding a debt a great shame.

But now she knew that she must do it, or let

those children perish; being herself old and past work, and having seen all her sons die out in their strength before her.

The struggle was long and hard with her.

She would have to die soon, she knew, and she had striven all her lifetime so to live that she might die saying, "I have asked nothing of any man."

This perhaps, she thought sadly, had been only a pride after all; a feeling foolish and wicked, that the good God sought now to chasten.

Any way she knew that she must yield it up and go and ask for something; or else those four small things, that were like a cluster of red berries on a leafless tree, must suffer and must perish.

"It is bitter, but I must do it," she thought. "Sure it is strange that the good God cares to take any of us to himself through so sharp a way as hunger. It seems, if I saw His face now, I should say, 'Not heaven for me, Monseigneur: only bread and a little wood.'"

And she rose up on her bent stiff limbs, and went to the pile of hay on which the children were lying, pale and thin, but trying to smile, all of them, because they saw the tears on her cheeks.

"Be still, my treasures," she said to them,

striving to speak cheerily, and laying her hands on the curls of the eldest born; "I go away for a little while to try and get you food. Be good, Bernardou, and take care of them till I come back."

Bernardou promised, being four years old himself; and she crept out of the little black door of the hut into the white road and the rushing winds.

"I will go to Flamma," she said to herself.

It was three in the afternoon, nearly dark at the season of midwinter. The business of the day was done.

The people had come and gone, favoured or denied, according to such sureties as they could offer.

The great wheel worked on in the seething water; the master of the mill sat against the casement to catch the falling light, adding up the sums in his ledger—crooked little signs such as he had taught himself to understand, though he could form neither numerals nor letters with his pen.

All around him in the storehouses there were corn, wood, wool, stores of every sort of food. All around him, in the room he lived in, there were hung the salt meats, the sweet herbs, and the dried fruits, that he had saved from the profusion of other and healthier years. It pleased him to know that he held all that, and also withheld it.

It moved him with a certain saturnine glee to see the hungry wistful eyes of the peasants stare longingly at all those riches, whilst their white lips faltered out an entreaty—which he denied. It was what he liked ; to sit there and count his gains after his fashion, and look at his stores and listen to the howling wind and driving hail, and chuckle to think how lean and cold and sick they were outside—those fools who had mocked him because his saint had been a gipsy's leman.

To be prayed to for bread, and give the stone of a bitter denial; to be implored with tears of supplication, and to answer with a grim jest ; to see a woman come with children dying for food, and to point out to her the big brass pans full of milk, and say to her "All that makes butter for Paris," and then to see her go away wailing and moaning that her child would die, and tottering feebly through the snow—all this was sweet to him.

Before his daughter had gone from him, he had been, though a hard man, yet honest, and had been, though severe, not cruel ; but since he had

been aware of the shame of the creature whom
he had believed in as an angel, every fibre in
him had been embittered and salted sharp with
the poignancy of an acrid hate towards all living
things. .To hurt and to wound, and to see what
he thus struck bleed and suffer, was the only
pleasure life had left for him. He had all his
manhood walked justly, according to his light, and
trusted in the God to whom he prayed ; and his
God and his trust had denied and betrayed him,
and his heart had turned to gall.

The old woman toiled slowly through the roads
which lay between her hut and the water-mill.

They were roads which passed through meadows
and along corn-fields, beside streamlets, and amongst
little belts of woodland, lanes and paths green
and pleasant in the summer, but now a slough of
frozen mud, and whistled through by north-east
winds. She held on her way steadily, stumbling
often, and often slipping and going slowly, for she
was very feeble from long lack of food, and the
intensity of the cold drove through and through
her frame.

Still she held on, bravely, in the teeth of the
rough winds and of the coming darkness, though
the weather was so wild that the poplar trees

were bent to the earth, and the little light in
the Calvary lamp by the river blew to and fro, and
at last died out. Still she held on, a little dark
tottering figure, with a prayer on her lips and a
hope in her heart.

The snow was falling, the clouds were driving
the waters were roaring, ·in the twilight : she was
only a little black speck in the vast grey waste
of the earth and the sky, and the furious air
tossed her at times to and fro like a withered
leaf. But she would not let it beat her ; she
groped her way with infinite difficulty, grasping a
bough for strength, or waiting under a tree for
breath a moment, and thus at last reached the
mill-house.

Such light as there was left showed her the
kitchen within, the stores of wood, the strings of
food ; it looked to her as it had looked to Phratos,
a place of comfort and of plenty ; a strong safe
shelter from the inclement night.

She lifted the latch and crept in, and went straight
to Claudis Flamma, who was still busy beneath the
window with those rude signs which represented to
him his earthly wealth.

She stood before him white from the falling snow,
with her brown face working with a strong emotion,

her eyes clear and honest, and full of an intense anxiety of appeal.

"Flamma," she said simply to him, "we have been neighbours fifty years and more—thou and I, and many have borrowed of thee to their hurt and shame, but I never. I am eighty-two, and I never in my days asked anything of man or woman or child. But I come to-night to ask bread of you,—bread for the four little children at home. I have heard them cry three days, and have had nothing to give them save a berry or two off the trees. I cannot bear it any more. So I have come to you."

He shut his ledger, and looked at her. They had been neighbours, as she had said, half a century and more; and had often knelt down before the same altar, side by side.

"What dost want?" he asked simply.

"Food," she made answer; "food and fuel. They are so cold—the little ones."

"What canst pay for them?" he asked.

"Nothing—nothing now. There is not a thing in the house except the last hay the children sleep on. But if thou wilt let me have a little—just a little—while the weather is so hard, I will find means to pay when the weather breaks. There is my garden; and I can wash and spin. I will pay faithfully. Thou knowest I never owed a brass coin to any man. But I am so old, and the children are so young——"

Claudis Flamma got up and walked to the other side of the kitchen. Her eyes followed him with wistful, hungry longing.

Where he went there stood pans of new milk, baskets of eggs, rolls of bread, piles of faggots. Her feeble heart beat thickly with eager hope, her dim eyes glowed with pleasure and with thankfulness.

He came back and brought to her a few sharp rods, plucked from a thorn tree.

"Give these to thy children's children," he said, with a dark smile. "For these—and for no more —will they recompense thee when they shall grow to maturity."

She looked at him startled and disquieted, yet thinking that he meant but a stern jest.

"Good Flamma, you mock me," she murmured, trembling; "the babes are little, and good. Ah, give me food quickly, for God's sake! A jest is well in season, but to an empty body and a bitter heart it is like a stripe."

He smiled, and answered her in his harsh grating voice,

"I give thee the only thing given without payment in this world—advice. Take it or leave it."

She reeled a little as if he had struck her a blow with his fist, and her face changed terribly, whilst her eyes stared without light or sense in them.

"You jest, Flamma! You only jest!" she muttered. "The little children starve, I tell you. You will give me bread for them? Just a little bread? I will pay as soon as the weather breaks."

"I can give nothing. I am poor, very poor," he answered her, with the habitual lie of the miser; and he opened his ledger again, and went on counting up the dots and crosses by which he kept his books.

His servant Pitchou sat spinning by the hearth: she did not cease her work, nor intercede by a word.

The poor can be better to the poor than any princes; but the poor can also be more cruel to the poor than any slave drivers.

The old woman's head dropped on her breast, she turned feebly, and felt her way, as though she were blind, out of the house and into the air.

It was already dark with the darkness of descending night.

The snow was falling fast. Her hope was gone : all was cold—cold as death.

She shivered and gasped, and strove to totter on : the children were alone. The winds blew and drove the snow flakes in a white cloud against her face ; the bending trees creaked and groaned as though in pain ; the roar of the millwater filled the air.

There was now no light : the day was gone, and the moon was hidden ; beneath her feet the frozen earth cracked and slipped and gave way.

She fell down ; being so old and so weakly she could not rise again, but lay still with one limb broken under her, and the winds and the storm beating together upon her.

"The children! the children!" she moaned feebly, and then was still : she was so cold, and the snow fell so fast ; she could not lift herself nor see what was around her ; she thought that she was in her bed at home, and felt as though she would soon sleep.

Through the dense gloom around her there came a swiftly moving shape; that flew as silently and as quickly as a night bird, and paused as though on wings beside her.

A voice that was at once timid and fierce, tender

and savage, spoke to her through the clouds of
driven snow spray.

"Hush, it is I! I—Folle - Farine. I have
brought you my food. It is not much—they never
give me much. Still it will help a little. I heard
what you said—I was in the loft. Flamma must
not know; he might make you pay. But it is all
mine, truly mine, take it."

"Food—for the children!"

The blessed word aroused her from her leth-
argy; she raised herself a little on one arm, and
tried to see whence the voice came that spoke
to her. But the effort exhausted her; she fell
again to the ground with a groan—her limb was
broken.

Folle-Farine stood above her; her dark eyes
gleaming like a hawk's through the gloom, and full
of a curious, startled pity.

"You cannot get up; you are old," she said,
abruptly. "See—let me carry you home. The
children! yes, the children can have it. It is not
much; but it will serve."

She spoke hastily and roughly; she was ashamed
of her own compassion. What was it to her,
whether any of these people lived or died? They
had always mocked and hated her.

"If I did right, I should let them rot, and spit on their corpses," she thought, with the ferocity of vengeance that ran in her oriental blood.

Yet she had come out in the storm, and had brought away her food for strangers, though she had been at work all day long, and was chilled to the bone, and was devoured with a ravenous hunger.

Why did she do it?

She did not know. She scorned herself. But she was sorry for this woman, so poor and so brave, with her eighty-two years, and so bitterly denied in her extremity.

Manon Dax dimly caught the muttered words, and feebly strove to answer them, whilst the winds roared and the snow beat upon her fallen body.

"I cannot rise," she murmured; "my leg is broken, I think. But it is no matter. Go you to the little ones; whoever you are, you are good, and have pity. Go to them, go. It is no matter for me. I have lived my life—any way. It will soon be over. I am not in pain—indeed."

Folle-Farine stood in silence a moment, then she stooped and lifted the old creature in her strong young arms, and with that heavy burden set out on her way in the teeth of the storm.

She had known the woman, and the little ones, by sight and name long and well.

Once or twice when she had passed by them, the grandam, tender of heart, but narrow of brain, and believing all the tales of her neighbours, had drawn the children closer to her, under the wing of her serge cloak, lest the evil eye that had bewitched the tanner's youngest born, should fall on them, and harm them in like manner.

Nevertheless the evil eyes gleamed on her with a wistful sorrow, as Folle-Farine bore her with easy strength and a sure step, through the frozen woodland ways, as she would have borne the load of wood, or the sack of corn, which she was so well used to carry to and fro like a pack-horse.

Manon Dax did not stir, she did not even strive to speak again; she was vaguely sensible of a slow, buoyant, painless movement, of a close soft pressure that sheltered her from the force of the winds, of a subtle warmth that stole through her emaciated aching frame, and made her drowsy and forgetful, and content to be still.

She could do no more. Her day for struggle and for work was done.

Once she moved a little. Her bearer paused and stopped and listened.

" Did you speak ? "

Manon Dax gave a soft troubled sigh.

" God is good," she muttered, like one speaking in a dream.

Folle-Farine held on her way, as before her Phratos had once held on his : fiercely blown, blinded by the snow, pierced by the blasts of the hurricane, but sure of foot on the ice as a reindeer, and sure of eye in the dark as a night-hawk.

" Are you in pain ? " she asked once of the burden she carried.

There was no answer.

" She is asleep," she thought ; and went onward.

The distance of the road was nothing to her, fleet and firm of step, and inured to all hardships of the weather ; yet it cost her an hour to travel it, heavily weighted as she was, soaked with snow-water, blown back continually by the opposing winds, and forced to stagger and to pause by the fury of the storm.

At last she reached the hut.

The wind had driven open the door. The wailing cries of the children echoed sorrowfully on the stillness, answered by the bleating of sheep, cold and hungry in their distant folds. The snow had drifted in unchecked ; all was quite dark.

She felt her way within over the heaps of the snow, and being used by long custom to see in the gloom, as the night-haunting beasts and birds can see, she found the bed of hay, and laid her burden gently down on it.

The children ceased their wailing; the two eldest ones crept up close to their grandmother; and pressed their cheeks to hers, and whispered to her eagerly, with their little famished lips:

" Where is the food, where is the food ? "

But there was still no answer.

The clouds drifted a little from the moon which had been so long obscured; it shone for a moment through the vapour of the heavy sky; the whitened ground threw back the rays increased tenfold; the pale gleam reached the old still face of Manon Dax.

There was a feeble smile upon it—the smile with which her last words had been spoken in the darkness; " God is good ! "

She was quite dead.

CHAPTER VI.

ALL that night Folle-Farine tarried with the children.

The youngest had been suffocated whilst they had been alone, by the snow that had fallen through the roof, from which its elders had been too small and weakly to be able to drag it out, unaided. She laid it, stiff already in the cold of the night, beside the body of its old grandam, who had perished in endeavouring to save it; they lay together, the year-old child and the aged woman, the broken bud and the leafless bough. They had died of hunger, as the birds die on the moors and plains; it is a common fate.

She stayed beside the children, who were frightened and bewildered and quite mute. She divided such food as she had brought between them, not taking any herself. She took off the sheepskin which she wore in winter tied round her loins as her out-door garment, and made a little nest of it for the three, and covered them with it. She could not close the door, from the height of the drifted snow, and the wind poured in all night. long, though in an hour the snow ceased to fall.

Now and then the clouds parting a little, let a ray of the moon stray in; and then she could see the quiet faces of the old dead woman and the child.

"They die of famine—and they die saying their 'God is good,'" she thought; and she pondered on it deeply, with the bitter and melancholy irony which life had already taught her.

The hours of the night dragged slowly on; the winds howled above the trembling hovel; the children sobbed themselves to sleep at last, lulled by the warmth of the sheepskin, in which they crept to-gether like young birds in a nest.

She sat there patiently; frozen and ravenous; yet not drawing a corner of the sheepskin to her own use, nor regretting a crumb of the bread she had surrendered.

She hated the human race, whose hand was always against her. She had no single good deed to thank them for, nor any single gentle word.

Yet she was sorry for that old creature, who had been so bitterly dealt with all her years through, who had died saying " God was good." She was sorry for those little helpless, unconscious starving animals, who had lost the only life that could labour for theirs.

She forgave—because she forgot—that in other winters this door had been shut against her as against an accursed thing, and these babes had mocked her in their first imperfect speech.

The dawn broke ; the sharp grey winter's day came ; the storm had lulled ; but the whole earth was frost-bound and white with snow, the air was piercing, the sky dark and overcast.

She had to leave them ; she was bound to her daily labour at the mill ; she knew that if when the sun rose she were found absent, she and they too would surely suffer. What to do for them she could not tell. She had no friend save Marcellin, who himself was as poor as these. She never spoke to any living thing, except a sheep-dog, or a calf bleating for its mother, or a toil-worn bullock staggering over the ploughed clods.

Between her, and all those around her, there were perpetual enmity and mistrust, and scarcely so much of a common bond as lies in a common

humanity.   For in her title to a common humanity
with them they disbelieved; while she in her scorn
rejected all claim to it.

At daybreak there passed by the open door in
the mist, a peasant going to his cattle in the fields
beyond, pushing through the snow a rude hand-cart
full of turnips, and other winter food.

She rose and called to him.

He stared and stood still.

She went to the doorway and signed to him.

" Old Manon Dax is dead.   Will you tell the
people ? The children are here, alone, and they
starve."

" Manon Dax dead ? " he echoed stupidly : he
was her nearest neighbour, and he had helped her
to fetch her washing-water sometimes from the well
half a league away, and when his wife had been
down, with fever and ague, the old woman had
nursed her carefully and well through many a
tedious month.

" Yes, I found her on the road, in the snow,
last night.   She had broken her leg, and she was
dead before I got here.   Go and send some one.
The little children are all alone, and one of them
is dead too."

It was so dark still, that he had not seen at first

who it was that addressed him, but slowly, as he stared and stared, and drew nearer to her, he recognised the scarlet girdle, the brown limbs, the straight brow, the fathomless eyes.

He feared her, with a great fear rising there suddenly before him, out of that still white world of dawn and shadow.

He dropped the handles of his cart and fled; a turn in the road, and the darkness of the morning, soon hid him from sight. She thought that he had gone to summon his people, and she went back and sat again by the sleeping children, and watched the sad still faces of the dead.

The peasant flew home as swiftly as his heavy shoes and the broken ice of the roads would allow.

His cabin was at some distance, at a place where, amidst the fields, a few huts, a stone crucifix, some barns and stacks, and a single wineshop made up a little village, celebrated in the district for its wide spreading orchards and their excellence of fruits.

Even so early the little hamlet was awake; the shutters were opened; the people were astir; men were brushing the snow from their thresholds; women were going out to their field-work; behind the narrow lattices the sleepy eyes and curly heads of children peered, while their fingers played with the fanciful encrustations of the frost.

The keeper of the tavern was unbarring his house door; a girl broke the ice in a pool for her ducks to get at the water; a few famished robins flew to and fro songless.

His own wife was on her doorstep; to her he darted.

"Manon Dax is dead!" he shouted.

"What of that?" said his wife, shouldering her broom; a great many had died that winter, and they were so poor and sharp-set with famine themselves, that they had neither bread nor pity to spare.

"This of that!" cried the old man, doggedly, and full of the excitement of his own terrors. "The young devil of Yprès has killed her, that I am sure. She is there in the hut in the dark, with her eyes glaring like coals. And for what should she be there if not for evil? Tell me that."

"Is it possible?" his wife cried, incredulous, yet willing to believe.

The girl left her ducks, the wineshop-keeper his door, the women their cabins, and came and stood round the bearer of such strange news: very welcome news in a raw frost-bitten dawn, when a day was beginning that would otherwise have had nothing more wonderful in it than tidings of how a litter of black pigs throve, and how a brown horse had fared with the swelling in the throat.

They were very dull there from year's end to year's end; once a month, may be, a letter would come in from some soldier-son or brother, or a pedlar coming to buy eggs would bring likewise some stray rumour from the outer world;—beyond this there was no change, they heard nothing, and saw nothing, seldom moving a league away from that stone crucifix, round which their little homes were clustered.

The man Flandrin had nothing truly to tell; he had fled horrified to be challenged, in the twilight and the snow, by a creature of such evil omen. But when he had got an audience, he was too true an orator and not such a fool as to lose it for such a little beggarly matter as the truth; and his tongue clacked quickly of all which his fears and fancies had conceived, until he had talked himself and his listeners into the full belief that Manon Dax being belated had encountered the evil glance of the daughter of all evil, and had been slain thereby in most cruel sorcery.

Now, in the whole neighbourhood, there was

nothing too foul to be credible of the begotten of the fiend—a fiend whom all the grown men and women remembered so well in his earthly form, when he had come to ruin poor Reine Flamma's body and soul, with his eyes like jewels, and his strength passing the strength of all men.

The people listened, gaping, and wonderstruck, and forgetting the bitterness of the cold, being warmed with those unfailing human cordials of foul suspicion and of gratified hatred. Some went off to their daily labour, being unable to spare time for more gossip ; but divers women who had nothing to occupy them remained about Flandrin.

A shrivelled dame, who owned the greatest number of brood-hens in the village, and who had only one son, a priest, and who was much respected and deferred to by her neighbours, spoke first when Flandrin had ended his tale for the seventh time, it being a little matter to him that his two hungry cows would be lowing all the while vainly for their morning meal.

" Flandrin, you have said well, beyond a doubt ; the good soul has been struck dead by sorcery. But, you have forgot one thing, the children are there, and that devil of Yprès is with them. We— good Christians and true—should not let such things be. Go, and drive her out and bring the young ones hither."

Flandrin stood silent.

It was very well to say that the devil should be driven out, but it was not so well to be the driver.

"That is as it should be," assented the other woman. "Go, Flandrin, and we—we will take the little souls in for this day, and then give them to the public charity, better cannot be done. Go."

"But mind that thou dost strike that beast, Folle-Farine, sharply!" cried his wife.

"If thou showest her the cross, she will have to grovel and flee," said another.

"Not she," grumbled the old dame, whose son was a priest. "One day my blessed son, who is nearly a saint, Heaven knows, menaced her with his cross, and she stood straight, and fearless, and looked at it, and said, 'By that sign you do all manner of vileness in this world, and say you are safe to be blest in another; I know!' and so laughed and went on. What are you to do with a witch like that,—eh?"

"Go, Flandrin," shrieked the women in chorus, "Go! Every minute you waste the little angels are nearer to hell!"

"Come yourselves with me, then," said Flandrin,

sullenly. "I will not go after those infants, it is not a man's work."

In his own mind he was musing on a story which his priests had often told him, of swine into which exorcised devils had entered, and despatched swiftly down a slope to a miserable end; and he thought of his own pigs, black, fat, and happy, worth so much to him in the market.

Better, he mused, that Manon Dax's grand-children should be the devil's prey, than those, his choicest, swine.

The women jeered him, menaced him, flouted him, besought him. But vainly—he would not move alone. He had become possessed with the terrors his own fancy had created; and he would not stir a step for all their imprecations.

"Let us go ourselves, then!" screamed his wife at length, flourishing above her head the broom with which she had swept the snow. "Men are ever cowards. It shall never be said of me, that I left those babes to the fiend while I gave my own children their porridge by the fire!"

There was a sentiment in this that stirred all her companions to emulation. They rushed into their homes, snatched a shovel, a staff, a broom, a pig-stick, each whatever came uppermost, and dragging

Flandrin in the midst, went down the sloping frozen road between its fringe of poplars.

They were not very sure in their own minds, why they went, nor for what they went; but they had a vague idea of doing what was wise and pious, and they had a great hate in their hearts against the child. They sped as fast as the slippery road would let them, and their tongues flew still faster than their feet; the cold of the daybreak made them sharp and keen on their prey, as the air was on themselves; they screamed fable on fable hoarsely, their voices rising shrilly above the whistling of the winds, and the creaking of the trees, and they inflamed each other with ferocious belief in the sorcery they were to punish.

They were in their way virtuous; they were content on very little; they toiled hard from their birth to their grave; they were most of them chaste wives and devoted mothers, they bore privation steadily, and they slaved in fair weather and foul without a complaint. But they were narrow of soul, greedy of temper, bigoted and uncharitable, and, when they thought themselves or their off-spring menaced, implacable.

They were of the stuff that would be burned for a creed, and burn others for another creed.

It is the creed of the vast majority of every nation; the priests and lawgivers of every nation have always told their people that it is a creed holy and honourable—how can the people know that it is at once idiotic and hellish?

Folle-Farine sat within on the damp hay under the broken roof, and watched the open door.

The children were still asleep. The eldest one in his sleep had turned and caught her hand, and held it.

She did not care for them. They had screamed, and run behind the woodstack, or their grandam's skirts, a hundred times when they had seen her on the road or in the orchard.

But she was sorry for them; almost as sorry as she was for the little naked woodpigeons when their nests were scattered on the ground in a tempest, or for the little starveling rabbits when they screamed in their holes for the soft white mother that was lying, tortured and twisted, in the jaws of a steel-trap.

She was sorry for them—half roughly, half tenderly sorry—with some shame at her own weakness, and yet too sincerely sorry to be able to persuade herself to leave them to their fate there, all alone with their dead. For in the savage heart of Taric's daughter there was an innermost corner wherein her mother's nature slept.

She sat there quite still, watching the porch, and listening for footsteps.

The snow was driven in encircling clouds by the winds; the dense fog of the dawn lifted itself off the surrounding fields; the branches of the trees were beautiful with hanging icicles; from the meadow hard-by there wailed unceasingly the mournful moaning of Flandrin's cattle, deserted of their master, and hungry in their wooden sheds.

She heard a distant convent clock strike six: no one came. Yet she had resolved not to leave the children all alone, though Flamma should come and find her there, and thrash her for her absence from his tasks. So she sat still, and waited.

After a little she heard the crisp cracking of many feet on the frozen snow and ice-filled ruts of the narrow road; she heard a confused clatter of angry voices breaking harshly on the stillness of the winter morning.

The light was stronger now, and through the doorway she saw the little passionate crowd of angry faces as the women pressed onward down the hill with Flandrin in their midst.

She rose, and looked out at them, quietly.

For a minute they paused—irresolute, silent, perplexed : at the sight of her they were half daunted ; they felt the vagueness of the crime they came to bring against her.

The wife of Flandrin recovered speech first, and dared them to the onslaught.

" What ! " she screamed, " nine good Christians fearful of one daughter of hell ?   Fie ! for shame ! Look ; my leaden Peter is round my neck !   Is he not stronger than she any day ? "

In a moment more, thus girded at and guarded at the same time, they were through the door and stood on the mud floor of the hearth, close to her, casting hasty glances at the poor dead body on the hearth, whose fires they had left to die out all through that bitter winter.

They came about her in a fierce, gesticulating, breathless troop, flourishing their sticks in her eyes, and casting at her all their various charges in one breath.   Flandrin stood a little aloof, sheepishly on the threshold, wishing that he had never said a word of the death of Manon Dax to his good wife and neighbours.

" You met that poor saint and killed her in the snow with your witcheries ! " one cried.

" You have stifled that poor babe where it lay ! "
cried another.

" A good woman like that ! " shrieked a third,
" who was well and blithe and praising God only a
day ago, for I saw her myself come down the hill
for our well water ! "

" It is as you did with the dear little Rémy, who
will be lame all his life, through you," hissed a
fourth. " You are not fit to live ; you spit venom
like a toad."

" Are you alive, my angels ? " said a fifth, waking
the three children noisily, and rousing their piercing
cries. " Are you alive after that witch has gazed on
you ? It is a miracle ! The Saints be praised ! "

Folle-Farine stood mute and erect for the moment,
not comprehending why they thus with one accord
fell upon her. She pointed to the bodies on the
hearth, with one of those grave and dignified gestures which were her birthright from the old
oriental race.

" She was cold and hungry," she said curtly, her
mellow accent softening and enriching the provin-
cial tongue which she had learned from those
amidst whom she dwelt. " She had fallen, and was
dying. I brought her here. The young child was
killed by the snow. I stayed with the rest because

they were frightened, and alone. There is no more to tell. What of it ?"

"Thou hadst better come away. What canst thou prove ?" whispered Flandrin to his wife.

He was afraid of the storm he had invoked, and would fain have stilled it. But that was beyond his power. The women had not come forth half a league in the howling winds of a midwinter daybreak only to go back [with a mere charity done, and with no vengeance taken.

They hissed, they screamed, they hurled their rage at her; they accused her of a thousand crimes; they filled the hut with clamour as of a thousand tongues ; they foamed, they spat, they struck at her with their sticks ; and she stood quiet, looking at them, and the old dead face of Manon Dax which lay upward in the dim light.

The eldest boy struggled in the grasp of the peasant woman who had seized him, and stretched his arms, instead, to the one who had fed him, and whose hand he had held all through his restless slumber in that long and dreary night. The woman covered his eyes with a scream.

"Ah——h !", she moaned, "see how the innocent child is bewitched ! It is horrible !"

"Look on that ;—oh, infernal thing !" cried

Flandrin's wife, lifting up her treasured figure of Peter. "You dare not face that blessed image. See—see all of you—how she winces, and turns white!"

Folle-Farine had shrunk a little as the child had called to her. Its gesture of affection was the first that she had ever seen towards her in any human thing.

She laughed aloud as the image of Peter was thrust in her face. She saw it was some emblem and idol of their faith, devoutly cherished. She stretched her hand out, wrenched it away, trampled on it, and tossed it through the doorway into the snow, where it sank and disappeared. Then she folded her arms, and waited for them.

There was a loud shriek at the blasphemy of the impious act; then they rushed on her.

They came inflamed with all the fury which abject fear and bigoted hatred can beget in minds of the lowest and most brutal type. They were strong, rude, ignorant, fanatical peasants, they abhorred her, they believed no child of theirs safe in its bed while she walked abroad alive. Beside such women, when in wrath and riot, the tiger and the hyæna are as the lamb and the dove.

They set on her with furious force, flung her,

R 2

trod on her, beat her, kicked her with their wood-shod feet, with all the malignant fury of the female animal that fights for its offspring's and its own security.

Strong though she was, and swift, and full of courage, she had no power against the numbers who had thrown themselves on her, and borne her backward by dint of their united effort, and held her down to work their worst on her.

She could not free herself nor return their blows, nor lift herself to wrestle with them; she could only deny them the sweetness of wringing from her a single cry, and that much she did.

She was mute while the rough hands flew at her, the sticks struck at her, the heavy feet were driven against her body, the fingers clutched at her long hair, and twisted and tore at it—she was quite mute throughout.

" Prick her in the breast, and see if the devil be still in her.   I have heard say there is no better way to test a witch ! " cried Flandrin's wife, writhing in rage for the outrage to the Petrus.

Her foes needed no second bidding ; they had her already prostrate in their midst, and a dozen eager hands seized a closer grip upon her, pulled her clothes from her chest, and, holding her down on the mud floor, searched with ravenous eyes for the signet marks of hell.

The smooth skin baffled them; its rich and tender hues were without spot or blemish.

"What matter; what matter?" hissed Rose Flandrin. "When our fathers hunted witches in the old time, did they stop for that? Draw blood, and you will see."

She clutched a jagged rusty nail from out the wall, and leaned over her prey.

"It is the only babe that will ever cling to thee!" she cried, with a laugh, as the nail drew blood above the heart.

Still Folle-Farine made no sound and asked no mercy.

She was powerless, defenceless, flung on her back amidst her tormentors, fastened down by treading feet and clenching hands; she could resist in nothing, she could not stir a limb, still she kept silence, and her proud eyes looked unquailing into the hateful faces bent to hers.

The muscles and nerves of her body quivered with a mighty pang, her chest heaved with the torture of indignity, her heart fluttered like a wounded bird—not at the physical pain, but at the shame of these women's gaze, the loathsome contact of their reckless touch. The iron pierced deeper, but they could not make her speak.

Except for her eyes, that glowed with a dusky fire as they glanced to and fro, seeking escape, she might have been a statue of olive wood, flung down by ruffians to make a bonfire.

"If one were to drive the nail to the head, she would not feel!" cried the women, in furious despair, and were minded, almost, to put her to that uttermost test.

Suddenly from the doorway Flandrin raised an alarm:

"There is our notary close at hand, on the road on his mule! Hist! Come out quickly. You know how strict he is, and how he forbids us ever to try and take the law into our own keeping. Quick—as you love your lives—quick!"

The furies left their prey, and scattered and fled, the notary was a name of awe to them, for he was a severe man, but just.

They seized the children, went out with them into the road, closed the hut door behind them, and moved down the hill; the children wailing sadly, and the eldest trying to get from them and go back.

The women looked mournful and held their

heads down, and comforted the little ones;
Flandrin himself went to his cattle in the
meadow.

"Is anything amiss?" the old white-haired
notary asked, stopping his favourite grey mule at
sight of the little cavalcade.

The women, weeping, told him that Manon Dax
was dead, and the youngest infant likewise—of cold,
in the night, as they supposed. They dared to say
no other thing, for he had many times rebuked
them for their lack of charity and their bigoted
cruelties and superstitions, and they were quaking
with fear lest he should by any chance enter the
cottage and see their work.

"Flandrin, going to his cow, saw her first, and
he came to us and told us," they added, crossing
themselves fervently, and hushing little Bernardou,
who wanted to get from them and return; "and we
have taken the poor little things to carry them
home; we are going to give them food, and warm
them awhile by the stove, and then we shall come
back and do all that is needful for the beloved dead
who are within."

"That is well. That is good and neighbourly of
you," said the notary, who liked them all, having
married them all, and registered all their children's

births, and who was a good old man though stern; kindly and very honest.

He promised them to see for his part that all needed by the law and by the church should be done for their old lost neighbour, and then urged his fat mule into a trot, for he had been summoned to a rich man's sick bed in that early winter morning, and was in haste lest the priest should be before-hand with him there.

"How tender the poor are to the poor! Those people have not bread enough for themselves, and yet they burden their homes with three strange mouths. Their hearts must be true at the core, if their tongues sometimes be foul," he mused, as he rode the mule down through the fog.

The women went on, carrying and dragging the children with them, in a sullen impatience.

"To think we should have had to leave that fiend of Yprès!" they muttered in their teeth. "Well, there is one thing, she will not get over the hurt for days. Her bones will be stiff for many a week. That will teach her to leave honest folk alone."

And they traversed the road slowly; muttering to one another.

"Hold thy noise, thou little pig!" cried

Flandrin's wife, pushing Bernardou on before her. "Hold thy noise, I tell you, or I will put you in the black box in a hole in the ground, along with thy great-grandmother."

But Bernardou wept aloud, refusing to be comforted or terrified into silence. He was old enough to know that never more would the old kindly withered brown face bend over him as he woke in the morning, nor the old kindly quavering voice croone him country ballads and cradle songs at twilight by the bright wood fire.

Little by little the women carrying the children crept down the slippery slope, half ice and half mud in the thaw, and entered their own village, and therein were much praised for their charity and courage.

For when they praise, as when they abuse, villages are loud of voice and blind of eye, much as are the cities.

Their tongues, and those of their neighbours, clacked all day long, noisily and bravely, of their good and their great deeds; they had all the sanctity of martyrdom, and all the glory of victory, in one.

True, they had left all their house and field work half done;—"but the Holy Peter will finish it in his own good time, and avenge himself for his outrage," mused the wife of Flandrin, sorrowing over her lost Petrus in the snowdrift, and boxing the ears of little Bernardou, as he huddled in her chimney corner, to make him cease from his weeping.

When they went back with their priest at noon to the hut of old Manon Dax to make her ready for her burial, they trembled inwardly lest they should find their victim there, and lest she should lift up her voice in accusation against them. Their hearts misgave them sorely. Their priest, a cobbler's son, and almost as ignorant as themselves, save that he could gabble a few morsels of bad Latin, would be, they knew, on their own side; but they were sensible that they had let their fury hurry them into acts which could easily be applauded by their neighbours, but not so easily justified to the law.

"For the law is over good," said Rose Flandrin, "and takes the part of all sorts of vile creatures. It will protect a rogue, á brigand, a bullock, a dog, a witch, a devil—anything,—except now and then an honest woman."

But their fears were groundless; she was gone; the hut when they entered it had no tenants except the lifeless famished bodies of the old grandam and the year-old infant.

When Folle-Farine had heard the hut door close,

and the steps of her tormentors die away down the hill, she had tried vainly several times to raise herself from the floor, and had failed.

She had been so suddenly attacked and flung down and trampled on, that her brain had been deadened, and her senses had gone for the first sharp moment of the persecution.

As she lifted herself slowly, and staggered to her feet, and saw the blood trickle where the nail had pierced her breast, she understood what had happened to her; and her face grew savage and dark, and her eyes fierce and lustful, like the eyes of some wild beast rising wounded in his lair.

It was not for the hurt she cared; it was the shame of defeat and outrage that stung her like a whip of asps.

She stood awhile looking at the dead face of the woman she had aided.

"I tried to help you," she thought. "I was a fool. I might have known how they pay any good done to them."

She was not surprised; her mind had been too deadened by a long course of ill usage to feel any wonder at the treatment with which she had been repaid.

She hated them with the mute unyielding hatred

of her race, but she hated herself more because she had yielded to the softness of sorrow and pity for any human thing; and more still because she had not been armed and on her guard, and had suffered them to prevail and to escape without her vengeance.

"I will never come abroad without a knife in my girdle again," she thought—this was the lesson that her charity had brought her as its teaching.

She went out hardening her heart, as she crept through the doorway into the snow and the wind, so that she should not leave one farewell word or token of gentleness with the dead, that lay there so tranquil on the ashes of the hearth.

"She lied, even in her last breath," thought Folle-Farine. "She said that her God was good!"

She could hardly keep on her own homeward way. All her limbs were stiff and full of pain. The wound in her chest was scarcely more than skin deep, yet it smarted sorely and bled still. Her brain was dull, and her ears were filled with strange noises from the force with which she had been flung backward on her head.

She had given her sheepskin to the children, as before her Phratos had done; and one of the peasants had carried the youngest away in it.

The sharpness of the intense cold froze the blood in her as she crawled through a gap in the poplar hedge, and under the whitened brambles and grasses, beyond, to get backward to the mill by the path that ran through the woods and pastures.

The sun had risen, but was obscured by fog, through which it shed a dull red ray here and there above the woods in the east.

It was a bitter morning, and the wind, though it had abated, was still rough, and drove the snow in clouds of powder hither and thither over the fields. She could only move very slowly, very stiffly; the thorns tearing her, the snow blinding her, the icicles lacerating her bare feet as she moved.

She wondered, dimly, why she lived. It seemed to her that the devil, when he had made her, must have made her out of sport and cruelty, and then tossed her into the world to be a scapegoat and a football for any creature that might need one.

That she might end her own life never occurred to her; her intelligence was not awake enough to see that she need not have borne its burden one hour more, so long as there had been one pool in the woods deep enough to drown her under its green weeds and lily leaves any cool summer night. Nay, —that she had but to lie down, then and there, where she was, beneath the ice-dropping trees, and let the sleep that weighed so heavily on her eye-lids come, dreamless and painless, and there would be an end of all for her, as for the frozen rabbits and the birds that strewed the upland meadows, starved and stiff.

She did not know;—and had she known, wretched though existence was to her, death would not have allured her. She saw that the dead might be slapped on their cheek, and could not lift their arm to strike again—a change that would not give her vengeance could have had no sweetness and no succour for her. The change she wanted was to live, and not to die.

By tedious and painful efforts, she dragged herself home by the way of the lanes and pastures; hungry, lame, bleeding, cold and miserable, with her eyes burning, and her hands and her head hot with fever.

She made her way into the mill-yard and tried to commence her first morning's work; the drawing of water from the well for the beasts and for the house, and the sweeping down of the old wide court round which the sheds and storehouses ran.

She never dreamed of asking either for food or pity, either for sympathy or remission of her labours.

She set to work at once, but for the only time since Phratos had brought her thither, the strength and vigour of her frame had been beaten.

She was sick and weak ; her hand sank off the handle of the windlass ; and she dropped stupidly on the stone edge of the well, and sat there leaning her head on her hands.

The mastiff came and licked her face tenderly. The pigeons left the meal flung to them on the snow, and flew merrily about her head in pretty fluttering caresses. The lean cat came and rubbed its cheek softly against her, purring all the while. The woman Pitchou saw her, and she called out of the window to her master.

" Flamma ! there is thy gad-about, who has not been a' bed all night."

The old man heard, and came out of his mill to the well in the courtyard.

" Where hast been ?" he asked sharply of her. " Pitchou says thou hast not lain in thy bed all night long. Is it so ?"

Folle-Farine lifted her head slowly, with a dazed stupid pain in the look of her eyes.

" Yes, it is true," she answered, doggedly.

" And where hast been then ?" he asked, through his clenched teeth ; enraged that his servant had been quicker of eye and of ear than himself.

A little of her old dauntless defiance gleamed in her face through its stupor and languor, as she replied to him with effort in brief phrases.

"I went after old Manon Dax, to give her my supper. She died in the road, and I carried her home. And the youngest child was dead too. I stayed there because the children were alone; I called to Flandrin and told him; he came with his wife and other women, and they said I had killed old Dax; they set on me, and beat me, and pricked me for a witch. It is no matter. But it made me late."

In her glance upward, even in the curtness of her words, there was an unconscious glimmer of appeal, a vague fancy that for once she might, perhaps, meet with approval and sympathy, instead of punishment and contempt. She had never heard a kind word from him, nor one of any compassion, and yet a dim unuttered hope was in her heart, that for once he might condemn her persecutors and pardon her.

But the hope was a vain one, like all which she had cherished since first the door of the mill-house had opened to admit her.

Flamma only set his teeth tighter. In his own soul he had been almost ashamed of his denial to his old neighbour, and had almost feared, that it would lose him the good will of that good heaven which had sent him so mercifully such a sharp year of famine to enrich him. Therefore, it infuriated him, to think that this offspring of a foul sin should have had pity and charity, where he had lacked them.

He looked at her and saw with grim glee, that she was black and blue with bruises, and that the linen which she held together across her bosom had been stained with blood.

"Flandrin and his wife are honest people, and pious," he said, in answer to her. "When they find a wench out of her bed at night, they deal rightly with her, and do not hearken to any lies that she may tell them of feigned alms-giving to cover her vices from their sight. I thank them that they did so much of my work for me. They might well prick thee for a witch; but they will never cut so deep into thy breast, as to be able to dig the mark of the devil out of it. Now, up and work, or it will be the worse for thee."

She obeyed him.

There during the dark winter's day, the pain

which she endured, with her hunger and the cold of the weather, made her fall thrice, like a dead thing, on the snow of the court, and the floors of the sheds. But she lay insensible till the youth in her brought back consciousness, without aid; in those moments of faintness, no one noticed her save the dog, who came and crept to her to give her warmth, and strove to wake her with the kisses of his rough tongue.

She did her work as best she might; neither Flamma nor his servant once spoke to her.

"My women dealt somewhat roughly with thy wench at break of day, good Flamma," said the man Flandrin, meeting him in the lane that afternoon, and fearful of offending the shrewd old man who had so many of his neighbours in his grip. "I hope thou wilt not take it amiss? The girl maddened my dame—spitting on her Peter, and throwing the blessed image away in a ditch."

"The woman did well," said Flamma, coldly, driving his grey mare onward through the fog.

Flandrin could not tell whether he were content, or were displeased.

Claudis Flamma himself, hardly knew which he was, himself; he held her as the very spawn of hell itself, and yet it was loathsome to him, that his neighbours should also know, and say, that a devil had been the only fruit of that fair offspring of his own, whom he and they had so long held as a saint.

The next day and the next, and the next again after that, she was too ill to stir ; they beat her and called her names, but it was of no use ; they could not get work out of her ; she was past it, and beyond all rousing of their sticks, or of .their words.

They were obliged to let her be. She stayed for nearly four days in the hay in her loft ; devoured with fever, and with every bone and muscle in pain. She had a pitcher of water by her and drank continually, thirstily, like a sick dog. With rest and no medicine but the cold spring water, she recovered : she had been delirious in a few of the hours, and had dreamed of nothing but of the old life in the Liébana, and of the old sweet music of Phratos. She remained there untended, shivering and fever-stricken, until the strength of her youth returned to her. She rose on the fifth day weaker, but otherwise little the worse; with the soft sad songs of her old friend the viol ringing always through her brain.

The fifth day from the death of Manon Dax, was the day of the new year.

There was no work being done at the mill; the
wheel stood still, locked fast, for the deep stream
was close bound in ice; frost had returned, and the
country was white with snow two feet deep, and
bleak and bare, and rioted over by furious cross
winds.

Flamma and Pitchou were in the kitchen
when she entered it; they looked up, but neither
spoke to her.　In being ill—for the first time since
they had had to do with her,—she had committed,
for the millionth time, a crime.

There was no welcome for her in that cheerless
place, where scarcely a spark of fire was allowed to
brighten the hearth, and where the hens, straying
in from without, sat with ruffled feathers, chilled
and moping, and where the old Black Forest clock
in the corner, had stopped from the intense
cold.

There was no welcome for her—she went out
into the air, thinking the woods, even at midwinter,
could not be so lonesome as was that cheerless
house.

The sun was shining through a rift in the stormy
clouds, and the white roofs, and the ice-crusted
waters, and the frosted trees, were glittering in its
light.

There were many dead birds about the paths. Claudis Flamma had thought their famine-time a good one, in which to tempt them with poisoned grain.

She wondered where the dog was who never had failed to greet her,—a yard farther on she saw him.

He was stretched stiff and lifeless beside the old barrel that had served him as a kennel; his master had begrudged him the little straw needful to keep him from the hurricanes of those bitter nights; and he had perished quietly, without a moan, like a sentinel slain at his post—frozen to death in his old age after a life of faithfulness repaid with blows.

She stood by him a while with dry eyes, but with an aching heart. He had loved her, and she had loved him; and many a time she had risked a stroke of the lash to save it from his body; and many a time she had sobbed herself to sleep in her earlier years, with her arms curled round him, as round her only friend and only comrade in bondage and in misery.

She stooped down; kissed him softly on his broad grizzled forehead, and lifted his corpse into a place of shelter, and covered it tenderly, so that he should not be left to the crows and the kites, until she should be able to make his grave in those orchards in which he had loved so well to wander, and in which he and she had spent all their brief hours of summer liberty and leisure.

She shuddered as she looked her last on him; and filled in the snow above his tomb, under the old twisted pear tree, beneath which, he and she had so often sat together in the long grasses, consoling one another for scant fare and cruel blows by the exquisite mute sympathy which can exist betwixt the canine and the human animal when the two are alone, and love and trust each other, only, out of all the world.

Whilst the dog had lived, she had had two friends; now that he slept for ever in the old grey orchard, she had but one left.

She went to seek this one.

Her heart ached for a kind glance—for a word that should be neither of hatred nor of scorn. It was seldom that she allowed herself to know such a weakness. She had dauntless blood in her; she came of a people that despised pity, and who knew how to live hard and to die hard, without murmur or appeal. Yet she had clung to the old mastiff, who was savage to all save herself; so she still clung to the old man Marcellin, who to all save herself was a terror and a name of foul omen.

He was good to her in his own fierce and rugged way; and they had the kinship of the proscribed; and they loved one another in a strange, silent, savage manner, as a yearling wolf cub and an aged grizzled bear might love each other in the depths of a forest, where the foot of the hunter and the fangs of the hound were alike against the young and the old.

She had not seen him for six days. She felt ill, and weak, and cold, and alone. She thought she would go to him in his hut, and sit a little by his lonely hearth, and hear him tell strange stories of the marvellous time when he was young, and the world was drunk with a mad sweet dream which was never to come true upon earth.

Her heart was in wild revolt, and a fierce futile hate gnawed ever in it. She had become used to the indignities of the populace, and the insults of all the people who went to and fro her grandsire's place; but each one pierced deeper and deeper than the last, and left a longer scar, and killed more and more of the gentler and better instincts which had survived in her through all the brutalising debasement of her life.

She could not avenge the outrage of Rose
Flandrin and her sisterhood, and being unable
to avenge it, she shut her mouth and said nothing
of it, as her habit was.   Nevertheless it festered
and rankled in her ; and now and then the thought
crossed her—why not take a flint and a bit of tow,
and burn them all in their beds as they slept in
that little hollow at the foot of the hill ?

She thought of it often—would she ever do it ?
She did not know.

It had a taint of cowardice in it ; yet a man that
very winter had fired a farmstead for far less an
injury, and had burned to death all who had lain
therein that night.   Why should she not kill and
burn these also ?   They had never essayed to teach
her to do better, and when she had tried to do good
to one of them, the others had set on her as a
witch.

In the afternoon of this first day of the year
she had to pass through their hamlet to seek
Marcellin.

The sun was low and red ; the dusky light
glowered over the white meadows and through the
leafless twilight of the woods ; here and there a
solitary tree of holly reared itself, scarlet and tall,
from the snowdrifts ; here and there a sheaf of

arrowy reeds pierced the sheets of ice that covered all the streams and pools.

The little village lay with its dark round roofs, cosy and warm, with all the winter round. She strode through it erect, and flashing her scornful eyes right and left; but her right hand was inside her skirt, and it gripped fast the handle of a knife. For such was the lesson which the reward for her charity had taught her—a lesson not lightly to be forgotten, nor swiftly to be unlearned again.

In its simple mode, the little place, like its greater neighbours, kept high festival for a fresh year begun.

Its crucifix rose, bare and white, out of a crown of fir boughs and many wreaths of ruddy berries. On its cabin windows the light of wood cracking and blazing within glowed brightly. Through them she saw many of their interiors as she went by in the shadow without.

In one the children knelt in a circle round the fire, roasting chestnuts in the embers with gay shouts of laughter. In another, they romped with their big sheep-dog, decking him with garlands of ivy and laurel.

In one little brown room a betrothal party made merry; in another, that was bright with Dutch tiles, and hung round with dried herbs and fruits, an old matron had her arm round the curly head of a sailor lad, home for a short glad hour.

In the house of Flandrin a huge soup-pot smoked with savoury odour, and the eyes of his wife were soft with a tender mirth as she watched her youngest-born playing with a Punch, all bells and bright colours, and saw the elder ones cluster round a gilded Jesus of sugar.

In the wine-shop, the keeper of it, having taken to himself a wife that day, kept open house to his friends, and he and they were dancing to the music of a horn and a fiddle, under rafters bedecked with branches of fir, with many-hued ribands, and with little oil lamps that blew to and fro in the noise of the romp. And all round were the dark still woods, and in the midst rose the crucifix; and above, on the height of the hill, the little old hut of Manon Dax stood dark and empty.

She looked at it all, going through it, with her hand on her knife.

" One spark," she thought, playing with the grim temptation that possessed her—" one spark on the dry thatch, and what a bonfire they would have for their feasting ! "

The thought was sweet to her.

Injustice had made her ravenous and savage. When she had tried to do well, and to save life, these people had accused her of taking it by evil sorcery.

She felt a longing to show them what evil indeed she could do, and to see them burn, and to hear them scream vainly, and then to say to them with a laugh, as the flames licked up their homes and their lives, " Another time, take care how you awake a witch ! "

Why did she not do it ? She did not know; she had brought out a flint and tinder in the pouch that hung at her side. It would be as easy as to pluck a sere leaf; she knew that.

She stood still and played with her fancy, and it was horrible and sweet to her—so sweet because so horrible.

How soon their mirth would be stilled !

As she stood thinking, there, and in her fancy seeing the red glare that would light up that peaceful place, and hearing the roar of the lurid flames that would drown the music, and the laughter, and the children's shouts, out of the twilight there rose to her a small dark thing, with a halo round its head : the thing was little Bernardou, and the halo was the shine of his curling hair in the lingering light.

He caught her skirts in his hands, and clung to her and sobbed.

"I know you—you were good that night. The people all say you are wicked, but you gave us your food, and held my hand. Take me back to gran'mère—oh, take me back!"

She was startled and bewildered.

This child had never mocked her, but he had screamed and run from her in terror, and had been told a score of stories that she was a devil, who could kill his body and soul.

"She is dead, Bernardou," she answered him; and her voice was troubled, and sounded strangely to her as she spoke for the first time to a child without being derided or screamed at in fear.

"Dead! What is that?" sobbed the boy. "She was stiff and cold, I know, and they put her in a hole; but she would waken, I know she would, if she only heard *us*. We never cried in the night but she heard in her sleep, and got up and came to us. Oh, do tell her—do, do tell her!"

She was silent; she did not know how to answer him, and the strangeness of any human appeal made to her bewildered her and held her mute.

"Why are you out in the cold, Bernardou?" she asked him suddenly, glancing backward through the lattice of the Flandrins' house, through which she could see the infants laughing and shaking the puppet with the gilded bells.

"They beat me; they say I am naughty, because I want gran'mère," he said, with a sob. "They beat me often, and oh! if she knew, she would wake and come. Do tell her—do! Bernardou will be so good, and never vex her, if only she will come back!"

His piteous voice was drowned in tears.

His little life had been hard; scant fare, cold winds, and naked limbs had been his portion; yet the life had been bright and gleeful to him, clinging to his grandam's skirts as she washed at the tub or hoed in the cabbage-ground, catching her smile when he brought her the first daisy of the year, running always to her open arms in any hurt, sinking to sleep always with the singing of her old ballads on his ear.

It had been a little life, dear, glad, kindly, precious to him, and he wept for it; refusing to be comforted by sight of a gilded puppet in another's hand, or a sugared Jesus in another's mouth, as they expected him to be.

It is the sort of comfort that is always offered to the homeless, and they are always thought ungrateful if they will not be consoled by it.

" I wish I could take you, Bernardou ! " Folle-Farine murmured, with a momentary softness that was exquisitely tender in its contrast to her haughty and fierce temper. " I wish I could."

For one wild instant the thought came to her to break from her bonds, and take this creature who was as lonely as herself, and to wander away and away into that unknown land which stretched around her, and of which she knew no more than one of the dark leaves knew that grew in the snow-filled ditch.

But the thought passed unuttered; she knew neither where to go nor what to do.

Her few early years in the Liébana were too dream-like and too vaguely remembered to be any guide to her ; and the world seemed only to her in her fancies as a vast plain, dreary and dismal, in which every hand would be against her, and every living thing be hostile to her. Beside, the long habitude of slavery was on her, and it is a yoke that eats into the flesh too deeply to be wrenched off without many an effort.

As she stood thinking, with the child's eager hands clasping her skirts, a shrill voice called from the wood-stack and dung-heap outside Flandrin's house :

" Bernardou ! Bernardou ! thou little plague. Come within. What dost do out there in the dark ? Mischief, I will warrant."

The speaker strode out, and snatched and bore and clutched him away ; she was the sister of Rose Flandrin, who lived with them, and kept the place and the children in order.

" Thou little beast ! " she muttered, in fury. " Dost dare talk to the witch that killed thy grandmother ? Thou shalt hie to bed, and sup on a fine whipping. Thank God, thou goest to the hospital to-morrow ! Thou wouldst bring a dire curse on the house in reward for our alms to thee."

She dragged him in and slammed-to the door, and his cries echoed above the busy shouts and laughter of the Flandrin family, gathered about the tinselled Punch and the sugared Jesus, and the soup-pot, that stewed them a fat farm-yard goose for their supper.

Folle-Farine listened awhile, with her hand clenched on her knife ; then she toiled onward through the village, and left it and its carols and carousings behind her in the red glow of the sinking sun.

She thought no more of setting their huts in a blaze ; the child's words had touched and softened her ; she remembered the long patient bitter life of the woman who had died of cold and hunger in her eighty-second year, and yet who had thus died saying to the last, " God is good."

" What is their God ? " she mused. " They care for him, and he seems to care nothing for them whether they be old or young."

Yet her heart was softened, and she would not fire the house in which little Bernardou was sheltered.

His was the first gratitude that she had ever met with, and it was sweet to her as the rare blossom of the edelweiss to the traveller upon the highest Alpine summits—a flower full of promise, born amidst a waste.

The way was long to where Marcellin dwelt, but she walked on through the fields that were in summer all one scarlet glow of poppies, and were now a white sheet of frozen water.

The day was over, the evening drew nigh, the sound of innumerable bells in the town echoed faintly from the distance, over the snow : all was still.

On the night of the new year the people had a care that the cattle in the byres, the sheep in the folds, the dogs in the kennels, the swine in the styes, the old cart-horses in the sheds, should have a full meal and a clean bed, and be able to rejoice.

In all the country round there were only two that were forgotten—the dead in their graves, and the daughter of Taric.

Folle-Farine was cold, hungry, and exhausted, for the fever had left her enfeebled; and from the coarse food of the mill-house her weakness had turned.

But she walked on steadily.

At the hut where Marcellin dwelt she knew that she would be sure of one welcome, one smile; one voice that would greet her kindly; one face that would look on her without a frown.

It would not matter, she thought, how the winds should howl and the hail drive, or how the people should be merry in their homes and forgetful of her and of him. He and she would sit together over the little fire, and give back hate for hate and scorn for scorn, and commune with each other, and want no other cheer or comrade.

It had been always so since he had first met her at sunset amongst the poppies, then a little child of eight years old. Every new-year's night she had spent with him in his hovel; and in

their own mute way they had loved one another,
and drawn closer together, and been almost
glad, though often pitcher and platter had been
empty, and sometimes even the hearth had been
cold.

She stepped bravely against the wind, and over
the crisp firm snow, her spirits rising- as she drew
near the only place that had ever opened its
door gladly to her coming; her heart growing
lighter as she approached the only creature
to whom she had ever spoken her thoughts
without derision or told her woes without con-
demnation.

His hut stood by itself in the midst of the wide
pastures, and by the side of a stream.

A little light was wont to twinkle at that hour
through the crevices of its wooden shutter; this
evening all was dark, the outline of the hovel rose
like a rugged mound against the white wastes round
it. The only sound was the far-off chiming of the
bells that vibrated strangely on the rarefied sharp
air.

She crossed the last meadow where the sheep
were folded for the night, and went to the
door and pushed against it to open it—it was
locked.

She struck it with her hand.

"Open, Marcellin—open quickly. It is only I."

There was no answer.

She smote the wood more loudly, and called to him again.

A heavy step echoed on the mud floor within; a match was struck, a dull light glimmered; a voice she did not know muttered drowsily, "Who is there?"

"It is I, Marcellin," she answered. "It is not night. I am come to be an hour with you. Is anything amiss?"

The door opened slowly, an old woman, whose face was strange to her, peered out into the dusk. She had been asleep on the settle by the fire, and stared stupidly at the flame of her own lamp.

"Is it the old man, Marcellin, you want?" she asked.

"Marcellin, yes—where is he?"

"He died four days ago. Get you gone; I will have no tramps about my place."

"Died!"

Folle-Farine stood erect, without a quiver in her face or in her limbs; but her teeth shut together like a steel clasp, and all the rich and golden hues of her skin changed to a sickly ashen pallor.

"Yes, why not?" grumbled the old woman. "To be sure men said that God would never let him die, because he killed St. Louis; but myself I never thought that. I knew the devil would not wait more than a hundred years for him—you can never cheat the devil, and he always seems stronger than the saints—somehow. You are that thing of Yprès, are you not? Get you gone!"

"Who are you? Why are you here?" she gasped.

Her right hand was clenched on the door-post, and her right foot was set on the threshold, so that the door could not be closed.

"I am an honest woman and a pious; and it befouls me to dwell where he dwelt," the old peasant hissed in loud indignation. "I stood out a whole day, but when one is poor, and the place is offered quit of rent, what can one do?—and it is roomy and airy for the fowls, and the priest has flung holy water about it and purified it, and I have a Horse-shoe nailed up, and a St. John in the corner. But be off with you, and take your foot from my door."

Folle-Farine stood motionless.

"When did he die; and how?" she asked in her teeth.

"He was found dead on the road, on his heap of stones, the fourth night from this," answered the old woman, loving to hear her own tongue, yet dreading the one to whom she spoke. "Perhaps he had been hungered, I do not know; or more likely the devil would not wait any longer; anyways, he was dead—the hammer in his hand. Max Liében, the man that travels with the wooden clocks, found him. He lay there all night. Nobody would touch him. They say they saw the mark of the devil's claws on him. At last they got a dung-cart, and that took him away before the sun rose. He died just under the great Calvary—it was like his blasphemy. They have put him in the common ditch. I think it shame to let the man that slew a saint be in the same grave with all the poor honest folk who feared God, and were Christians though they might be beggars and outcasts. Get you gone, you be as vile as he. If you want him go ask your father the foul fiend for him—they are surely together now."

And she drove the door to, and closed it, and barred it firmly within.

"Not but what the devil can get through the

chinks," she muttered, as she turned the wick of her lamp up higher.

Folle-Farine went back over the snow; blind, sick, feeling her way through the twilight as though it were the darkness of night.

"He died alone—he died alone," she muttered, a thousand times, as she crept shivering through the gloom; and, she knew, that now her own fate was yet more desolate. She knew that now she lived alone without one friend on earth.

The death on the open highway; the numbness, and stillness, and deafness to all the maledictions of men; the shameful bier made at night on the dung-cart, amidst loathing glances and muttered curses; the nameless grave in the common ditch with the beggar, the thief, the harlot, and the murderer;—these, which were so awful to all others, seemed to her as sweet as to sink to sleep on soft unshorn grass, whilst rose leaves are shaken in the wind, and fall as gently as kisses upon the slumberer.

For she in her youth and in the splendour of her strength, and in the blossom of her beauty, gorgeous as a passion-flower in the sun, envied bitterly the old man who had died at his work on the public road, hated by his kind, and weighted with the burden of nigh a hundred years.

Since his death was not more utterly lonely and desolate than was her life; and to all taunts and to all curses the ears of the dead are deaf.

END OF VOL. I.

BRADBURY, EVANS, AND CO., PRINTERS, WHITEFRIARS.

Im The Story

personalised classic books

"Beautiful gift... lovely finish.
My Niece loves it, so precious!"

Helen R Brumfieldon

★★★★★

UNIQUE GIFT

FOR KIDS, PARTNERS
AND FRIENDS

Timeless books such as:

Kids

Alice in Wonderland • The Jungle Book • The Wonderful Wizard of Oz
Peter and Wendy • Robin Hood • The Prince and The Pauper
The Railway Children • Treasure Island • A Christmas Carol

Adults

Romeo and Juliet • Dracula

Highly
Customizable

Change
Books Title

Replace
Characters Names
with yours

Upload
Photo into
inside page

Add
inscriptions

Visit

Im The Story .com

and order yours today!